It Hit Me Like a Ton of Bricks

NORTH POINT PRESS

A DIVISION OF FARRAR, STRAUS AND GIROUX • NEW YORK

It Hit Me Like a Ton of Bricks

A MEMOIR OF A MOTHER AND DAUGHTER

CATHERINE LLOYD BURNS

NORTH POINT PRESS
A division of Farrar, Straus and Giroux
19 Union Square West, New York 10003

Distributed in Canada by Douglas & McIntyre Ltd.
Printed in the United States of America
First edition, 2006

Library of Congress Cataloging-in-Publication Data
Burns, Catherine Lloyd.
    It hit me like a ton of bricks : a memoir of a mother and
daughter / Catherine Lloyd Burns.— 1st ed.
        p.   cm.
    ISBN-13: 978-0-86547-708-7 (hardcover : alk. paper)
    ISBN-10: 0-86547-708-6 (hardcover : alk. paper)
    1. Burns, Catherine Lloyd. 2. Actors—United States—
Biography. 3. Mothers and daughters—New York (State)—New
York—Biography.   I. Title.

PN2287.B86A3 2006
792.02'8092—dc22

                                                    2005025474

Designed by Gretchen Achilles

www.fsgbooks.com

10 9 8 7 6 5 4 3 2 1

My mother said, "When am I going to read it?"

"When I'm done," I said.

"Are you being *sensitive* to my *sensitivities*? I hope."

"I told you, it is a very three-dimensional, realistic portrait. Of both of us. I probably come off worse than you do."

"Well I think you should write a *disclaimer*," she said, "which clearly states there are *three* truths: *mine*, yours, and the *truth*."

This book is dedicated to my mother. And to my daughter, who I hope will be sensitive to my sensitivities when the time comes.

Also for RM.

Part One

SOMETHING NICE ABOUT
MY MOTHER

My answering machine is ablaze. I have sixteen messages, all from her. She needs to see me right away. What a pain in the ass. She lives in the Village. I live in Harlem. "Please hurry," she begs.

I walk in her front door an hour and a half later. She is in tears. I have been her daughter for nineteen years and this is the first time I have ever seen her cry. I don't like it. I thought I would like it. I concentrate on hanging up my vintage faux fur coat. "I thought you were dead," she tells my back.

"Well I'm not," I say. She leads me to the living room, to the center of the U made by her three white Knoll sofas. There are tissues everywhere. She is shaking, clinging to me.

Oh my God, I think, *this is it. This is the moment I have steered my whole little life toward.*

"I'm so glad to see you," she says, blowing her nose. "I thought you were dead. I was terrified you were dead."

"I'm not," I repeat.

"And then it hit me like a ton of bricks."

I sit down next to her. *She is going to reach out to me. She is going to apologize.* I look into her bloodshot blue eyes.

"It suddenly hit me today," she says. "I don't know why, but it hit me like a ton of bricks. This has nothing to do with me. If you kill yourself, it is simply not my fault. I am off the hook. None of this is my fault. I am not responsible." She looks almost euphoric as she takes my hand. "And I couldn't wait to tell you."

I am the chef, the star, the main ingredient. My mother is just the assistant. She explains what I do to the camera. "Cathy will pour the egg into the bowl," or "Cathy will now mix." Julia Child is also a chef and personality on TV. Julia Child throws all her garbage on the floor, which my mother cannot believe. I want to throw all our garbage on the floor too, but we are allowed to throw our garbage only in the sink, not on the floor like Julia Child. I also like how on Julia Child's show the finished recipe is always waiting, fully baked, bubbling, and brown, in the oven. It makes her show very professional. I wish our show were that professional. But, as my mother points out, our show is just a game.

My mother says, "Oh I'll just put my bagel right here while I go answer the phone." She is not saying it to me, because I am not here. I am invisible. I am hiding behind this chair. I gaze at the buttery golden brown perfectly toasted bagel. I can smell the yeast from across the kitchen. When the coast is clear I take it—plate, napkin, and all—and creep out of the room. This is the life I am forced to live because the food my mother makes for herself tastes significantly better than the food she makes for me.

"Don't be ridiculous, Cathy, it's the same bagel," she said when I told her.

"No. Yours is better. It has better butter. You try. Taste."

"There is no difference."

"Yes. Really."

"Don't be ridiculous, Cathy," my mother said, ending the conversation. But I won't give in. We argue until she backs down. This is the plan: from now on she will pretend all food prepared for me is really for her and then I will steal it when she isn't looking. This is the only way I can be certain of the quality. I take a bite of my freshly stolen bagel. It's good, but not amazing. The plan is sound. But her heart isn't in it.

My mother wraps my hair in a towel after my bath and says, "Well, Lady Josephine, what do you have to say for yourself?" It is like magic the way she gets the towel to stay on top of my head. Even though it's twirled around and around so many times, it never falls off. She carries me all the way down the green carpeting to my room. She tucks me in and says, "Good night, blessing." She pats my hair until I fall asleep but I don't let myself fall asleep because I don't want her to stop. Ever. Nannies don't do this. They say I am too old.

This is another game.

"What do you say, Cathy. Dog or *dawg*?"

"Dog."

"Very good. Now do you say, *I wanna cuppa wooda* or I want a cup of water?"

"I want a cup of water."

"Good. *Cawfee* or coffee?"

"Coffee." I am four but I win every time.

"I don't want you to end up like a truck driver," my mother says. "It's my biggest fear for you. Those New York accents are just terrible."

My mother is from Canada. They don't have those terrible accents there.

My mother has a black shiny alligator purse with a big gold *H* on the front. It smells like mint and leather and the bottom is soft from strands of tobacco. When you open and close it, it makes a clicking noise that is very good. In her top drawer are rows and rows of black velvet boxes with pins made of jewels in the shape of flowers and bugs. I pry open every lid until I find the butterfly. She has a watch in there too, made of real gold and real diamonds. My father gives her these things, and fur coats, and endless bottles of limited-edition Joy perfume, and she says she hates them. In his top drawer is a beige suede pouch filled with cuff links. He has hundreds of them: smooth ones, shiny ones, bumpy ones, gold ones, silver ones, ones with jewels, ones with ridges. My father travels a lot for his job. My mother used to have a job, but now she travels with my father instead because he is old-fashioned and a male chauvinist. Before she met him she was poor but now they are comfortable.

We live on Park Avenue and Sixty-first Street. I am pretty sure we are rich. We used to live on Central Park West and Ninety-first Street, until my father decided it was no place "to raise women and children" because my brother saw a holdup with a gun on his way home from school. My mother's first husband died when she was twenty-eight and my brother and sister were six and three. Seven years later she married my father. He brought a daughter from his first marriage who was sixteen. I was born right after their second anniversary. My brother and sisters are my half brother and sisters, but I don't call them that.

I sit on my parents' bed, in a fort made of clothes, watching my mother pack. I press the crisp cuffs of my father's shirts between my fingers and pray that he will go alone on this trip and leave my mother here with me. And then I worry I will burn in hell for wishing my own father would go away. The night before they come back I make a welcome-home sign for the front door. They always bring me a doll in native dress. The dolls are hard, not cuddly. You can't take their clothes off and only their arms move so you can't make them do anything. I don't like them. But I guess their outfits are interesting. I have France, Spain, Japan, China, Thailand, Switzerland, Australia, Greece, Canada, and Mexico.

My father works for Screen Gems in foreign distribution. Fernando Rey comes for drinks and crabmeat dip, which is pink and made out of ketchup and mayonnaise. I am allowed to stir it with the fork. It tastes good. Sean Connery sent roses to my middle sister for her sixteenth birthday. He is not a Screen Gems star, just a friend. I wish the Monkees were our friends so they could come over. I wish the Flying Nun would come over. My father has a picture of himself with her. And with Elizabeth Montgomery. And with Barbara Eden, except she isn't wearing her *I Dream of Jeannie* costume in the picture so she doesn't look that good. I have a photo album of him posing with all the stars from the Screen Gems lineup. I love TV. I dress up to watch TV because the people on TV get dressed up for me so it seems fair. There are also lots of pictures of my parents on their trips; getting off of planes, walking down runways, being greeted by little Japanese girls holding boxes of roses and dressed like one of my souvenir dolls. My mother always wears a fur coat and sunglasses and a scarf. She looks as good as the people on TV.

Evelyn is a nanny. Evelyn's name is hard to say. I have no control over Evelyn's name when it comes out of my mouth. Evelyn always says, "Wait till your mother comes home."

"I'm thirsty, Elvelyn."

"Wait till you mother comes home."

"I'm cold. Can I have a sweater?"

"Wait till your mother comes home."

"Can I have a snack, Elevyn?"

"Wait till your mother comes home."

Evelyn wears a uniform. Once I saw her without it. It was embarrassing. Evelyn always closes my door all the way. I tell her to leave it open a little bit, but she never does. She thinks everything I ask for is going to get her into trouble. I am in my room and I am supposed to take a nap but I'm not going to because I am too nervous about breathing up all the air before my nap is over and dying of suffocation because the door is closed.

"ELEVYN!" I scream at the top of my lungs, but only once because I don't want to get winded. If I get winded I'll breathe harder and use up the air sooner, and die faster.

On the other side of the door I hear Evelyn say, "Wait till your mother comes home."

"My *mother* is in *Europe*. She's not coming home for two more weeks. I'm sure she doesn't want me to suffocate!" I say. But I am just talking to a closed door. I can hear Evelyn's feet. They are already walking down the hall. I hate Evelyn.

My mother only lets me wear navy blue. Navy brings out my eyes. She can't buy anything for me unless it is navy. Sometimes a saleslady does not know this and will show us something in green or red.

"We'll take the navy," my mother instructs.

"*Please* can I have red?" I ask. My mother ponders the implications of this request while the saleslady and I wait. "No," my mother finally says. "We'll take the navy. The navy brings out your eyes. It brings out her eyes."

I am nine. My parents are in Tokyo and London. My sister is in charge. She is always in a good mood. She lets me have cookies for breakfast. They leave her with thousands of cash dollars. She pays the nanny, the maid, the butcher, and the baker. We take taxis everywhere. The big wrought-iron door at my school opens at three o'clock. I am watching this one say goodbye to that one, that one tease another one, someone else borrow money for the Good Humor man. The air is clear as a bell. The cherry blossoms are in bloom, the sun is bright, and there are birds chirping all over the place. It is a Technicolor New York City day, until my sister appears halfway down the block.

"What are you doing here? I don't get picked up anymore. I am allowed to go home by myself." I rail at her, daring her to come closer. She is going to embarrass me in front of my friends, I can tell.

"I have to tell you something. Something bad happened," she keeps coming toward me. "It's about Daddy."

"What, he's dead?" I say the most ridiculous thing I can think of.

"Yes," she says. Her face is the color of cement. "He died this morning." Everything turns to filth. I am covered in soot. I want to go back. Five minutes. Not even five minutes. Just to right before I said it.

"I didn't mean it. I was kidding. I didn't mean it!" I am shouting but no sound comes out. My sister picks me up and carries me like a baby. I am high above all the other kids. I can see the tops of their heads. We turn left onto Fifth Avenue and get in a taxi. I can't breathe. I want my mother. Our apartment is filled with adults, people I don't know who think they know me. I want my mother. She's still in London where my father died. I can see her in Toronto at the funeral.

"What's the funeral?" I ask my brother because he usually tells the truth and I happen to be alone with him in the pantry. He flew home this morning from college.

"Oh," he says. "It's where the dead person is."

"Papa will be there?"

"Well sort of. He'll be in a coffin," he says.

"What's a coffin?"

"It's like a box they put the dead person in so they can bury it in the ground."

"Oh," I say.

"I wouldn't go if I didn't have to," he tells me. He messes up my hair with his hand. We stand there for a minute. He does it again and then he leaves.

"I don't want to go," I tell my mother when she calls from London. I stay in New York with a nanny who used to look after me until she got married and had her own child. I know my father is dead. But I still think he will come home. I decide if I can walk down the hall, all the way to the bathroom, in four giant steps, he will come back. If I drink a whole glass of milk without putting it down, he will come back. If I get to the corner before a light turns red, he will come back. I want to make it happen before everyone comes home from the funeral.

I imagine their stunned faces as they open the front door and I say, "Look who's here." Everyone will hug me. I will be the hero. I will have saved my family. My father will be the happiest of all.

At school all the kids in my class wait for me on the stairs. They know my father died. They tell me they know because there was an article in the paper.

I ask my mother to show me the article. She doesn't know what I'm talking about. I say the kids at school told me it was there. She says, "Oh for Christ's sake, the obituary? Is that what you're talking about? It's not an article." She hands me the paper open to the page. I scour the tiny little blurb. There is no picture, no description of his life or accomplishments, and they spelled my name with a *K*. It is totally anticlimactic.

At night I don't sleep. I can't. I'm on watch. I stare into the dark and wait for his return. A month goes by. He's still dead. When I do sleep I dream they ask me to leave my school.

"It's not that we don't like you, it's just that your father . . ." my teacher says very kindly and then can't seem to finish his sentence.

"Is dead?" I offer.

"Yes," he tells me softly. I never blame him. I can tell he didn't make up the rule.

"Well," my mother says all the time, "you're lucky you had a good father for nine years. Some people have rotten fathers for the rest of their lives. You're very lucky. *I* think what must be really hard is having two parents alive that are divorced. *That* would be terrible."

"Oh," I say. I want to believe her.

I decide my father is in Heaven. He's dead but he's awake and it is sunny. But I still want him to come home.

"I miss him," I tell her one day when she catches me crying in my room.

"Listen very carefully to me," my mother says. "This is *very* important. Are you listening? You can use this to make people feel sorry for you. Don't do that. Don't be manipulative. Manipulative people are no good. I don't care for manipulative people."

She also tells me I was too smart for him. "That man loved you no matter what you did. You were like a little miracle to him. You could have killed someone and he still would have loved you. But you knew better than that. You knew you had to earn love. You don't just get love for nothing."

My mother is forty-five. The first time she was a widow she was twenty-eight. She cried into her pillow every night, she had two kids and a mortgage, and she was so broke she had to take in boarders. She carried on with a man named Sterling Jackson who was no good. My six-year-old brother threw his dinner that she could not afford across the floor one night and yelled at her, "You don't even miss him!" Her in-laws bought her a car. They didn't like how she parked it. They said when she could afford to pay her own parking tickets she could park sloppy, but for now, they said, go move the car. She says she looked out the window and decided she would never be dependent on anyone again as long as she lived. "The seasons change. Death is a part of life. Nothing lasts. You are born and you die. Everything is cyclical," my mother says, patting my hair. "If things are good, enjoy them," she tells me, pulling my blanket up, "because it ain't gonna last."

THE WHITE CLAPBOARD HOUSE

My mother rents a white clapboard house in Aspen the next summer. In exchange for free rent and groceries, my twenty-four-year-old brother and my twenty-one-year-old sister have to look after me, their ten-year-old sister. I fly by myself to Denver. It's okay. It's a jet. I like jets. It is the flight to Aspen from Denver that is always bad. It is not a jet. My brother meets me in Denver and flies the rest of the way with me. As usual, I heave into the white plastic-lined paper bag with the cardboard tabs the whole time. My brother moves to another row. I have one friend in Aspen. Her father owns the Jerome Hotel. He lets us hang out by the pool all day for free and snoop in the empty rooms. But she went to tennis camp in Michigan this summer instead.

My brother and sister buy lots of pot and records. My brother is trying to expand my sister's musical repertoire. He wants her to move beyond the Beatles and the Rolling Stones and Bob Dylan and Simon and Garfunkel so she can experience the flavors of *The Low Spark of High Heeled Boys*, *Workingman's Dead*, *Delaney and Bonnie*, and the Laura Nyro album with LaBelle. (But only the album with LaBelle; he is very strict about this. Laura Nyro by herself is no good.) My sister has been buying pot since I can remember. The shelves in her room on Park Avenue were stacked with clear plastic boxes in different colors from Azuma filled with pot, seeds, rolling papers, roaches, and roach clips. She's very organized. When I was eight she gave me a book called *A Child's Garden of Grass* because she said she wanted me to know what she was doing even though she couldn't do it with me for another ten years. She made my parents try it. My mother loved it and my father said he didn't get it.

In the late afternoons Randy Newman wails on about blowing up everything but Australia and the kangaroos. My brother croons along, head back, eyes closed, in complete agreement. At night my sister makes dinner and they argue about Livingston Taylor. My brother believes James is the only Taylor with enough talent to have a recording career; Livingston and Kate should get out of the business, he says, and get real jobs. We eat mostly spaghetti. It is sort of like all the other times we are on our own. Except this time my father is not in the Far East. He is dead. We do not talk about this.

Instead, they smoke joints all day and I ride my bike. I glide through puddles, watching the water fan out in a slow-motion V around my front wheel and play "Born to Be Wild" inside my head pretending that I am not a chicken through and through. A couple of weeks into June, a friendship is arranged for me with a boy and girl whose family rented a house nearby. Their parents knew my father. They are in show business. They smoke pot. There are always some famous people lying around naked on the back deck working on their tans. Jack Nicholson was there yesterday. We spy on them. We also write and stage cinema verité–style theater pieces. We make the adults put their clothes back on and be our audience. Our shows contain many complicated action sequences. It is necessary for the audience to run after us, otherwise they will miss important plot points. They trip and fall a lot because they are high and my friend's mother slows us down the most because the fringes of her embroidered shawls get caught on branches and outdoor furniture as she runs. Someone has to stop and untangle her, which messes up our show. We also kill time wandering up and down the aisles of the drugstore downtown. My friend and I look at makeup and candy while her brother spends hours slowly turning the covers of *Playboy* magazines, determined to find the right angle that will expose more boob. We call him "pervert" and run away. Sometimes they try and take my clothes off. They are a family and I am not. I wish I belonged to them, or to someone. No one's parents are ever as nice to me as I think they should be.

A famous singer comes to sunbathe. He is new in town. My sister is assigned the job of tour guide. They fall in love. He asks her to move in with him but she can't because she has to stay in the white clapboard house with me. The singer doesn't understand. The singer has hair that sticks straight up, like an Afro, but he is white and you can see the other side of the room through his blond hair.

"Come on, Michael," my sister says. Her beaded leather bag and her big, thick black hair are smushed under her body, against the door frame, for support. "I want to move in with Artie. I had her all of June and July. You do August."

"I don't know what to do with her all day. What am I supposed to do with a *kid* all day?" my brother says.

"Oh *Jesus*, you drop her off at the pool in the morning and you pick her up in the afternoon. How hard can it be? You haven't had her one *fucking* day since she got here." I feel like there is blood in my ears, rocks in my throat. Today was not the right day to skip my bike ride. My sister looks up and sees me. She takes me to the kitchen and smashes something up in a spoon with some honey and tells me to eat it.

"What is it?" I ask, as the gritty sweetness slides down.

"It's a Valium," she says. "It will make you feel better."

When I wake up my brother takes me away from the white clapboard house to live with him and two friends from college in an apartment on the other side of town. My sister has already moved in with the singer. The white clapboard house is empty. I feel sorry for the white clapboard house. My brother's friends are nice to me. They are a couple. They sleep in the same bed like my parents did. They listen to *Aerial Ballet* and Brewer & Shipley. There is a lot of kissing. A lot of pot. They always have the kind of doughnuts you buy from the supermarket. I really want a chocolate one, but I don't know if it is okay to eat that kind. Nobody told me what to eat for breakfast. I eat a gross cinnamon one because there is only one left and I think no one will notice it missing. I eat it and clean up all the crumbs and move all the other doughnuts around so it looks like a full box. I check it three times. It looks like nothing is missing. When my brother wakes up at noon he yells at me for eating the last cinnamon doughnut. "How could you do that? The reason there was only one left is because I like them the most. Now I have to eat a chocolate one. I hate chocolate!" He slams the refrigerator door for effect and goes back to bed, mad and doughnutless.

My mother calls long-distance to tell me that in spite of the recession and the fact that apartments cost a fortune she got us a sprawling three-bedroom in a prewar doorman building overlooking Washington Square Park. We are moving downtown. I am changing schools too. I burst into tears. My sister tells me not to worry because even though all the kids from my old school seem important now, one day, she says, I won't even remember their names. I tell her that's not true. I tell her I will always remember their names. She smiles at me like I am too young to know what I am saying. But I do know what I am saying. And I feel older than all of them.

I move in with my sister and the singer. The singer is learning to play the harpsichord. I am not allowed to touch the harpsichord. The singer's house is in the mountains and my sister can't spend all her time driving me around so I stay inside not touching the harpsichord and climbing up and down the shag-carpeted sunken living room. I play with the ice dispenser on the door of the fridge. I listen to *Blue*. The singer is impressed that I know all the words. I fly back to New York in August listening to "This Flight Tonight" on headphones. *Turn this crazy bird around. I shouldn't have got on this flight tonight,* Joni Mitchell sings.

GREENWICH VILLAGE

My mother has a boyfriend who wears hip-huggers and is pretentious. I may be eleven but I know an idiot when I meet one. They have a lot of sex. They aren't trying to hide it either. It is the grossest thing I have ever seen in my life. They look like ferocious little animals. I bring them coffee every morning. I don't know why. Maybe it is an attempt to make them behave responsibly, to get them to cut down on their morning fornication. I bring it to them on a tray, like a little servant girl. His cup always gets a big shake of Tabasco. They never say anything about it. He is younger than one of my sisters. He is disgusting.

It is freezing cold. We are walking home through Washington Square Park after pretending to say goodbye to him in front of a bunch of people they work with. I would pay money to say goodbye to him for good, forever. But five minutes after we get home the doorbell will ring and they will start humping each other again.

"Why don't you like Donny?" my mother asks me under the arch.

"Because he's gross."

"Well," she says. "You may not like him, but he's not gross."

"Then why are you ashamed of him?" I counter.

"I am not ashamed of him," she says.

"Oh really? Then how come he has to sneak over? Why are you too embarrassed to walk down the street with him?"

"I am not *embarrassed*, Cathy. It's very complicated. There are people I work with who wouldn't—he knows people that—it's very complicated. But I certainly don't have to explain it to you."

It is clear to me I won the argument. I should be a fucking *lawyer*.

I rock every day after school. I curl up in a ball and put my head in my hands, tuck my legs under my stomach, and rock back and forth. It's total bullshit. It is what crazy people do. I read it in *I Never Promised You a Rose Garden*. I am waiting for her to say something about it. My oldest sister calls from Canada all the time to tell me the worst thing you can do to a child is tell them that the way they feel isn't true. I don't like our new apartment. I miss Park Avenue. I miss the split-pea-green carpet in the hall, which was ugly but was the same carpet in my room and in my parents' room and in my sister's room. I miss the breakfast nook where my parents read *The New York Times* every morning and where my mother taught me about clothes. "Ach, have you ever seen such an awful dress, who would wear this? Look at this, Cathy, it is hideous." I miss the kitchen cabinets with the glass doors that went all the way to the ceiling and you could see what was inside and the glass was covered with psychedelic decals my sister stuck on the year before my father died. I miss my father, but I try not to think about that. I have two lives: one with a father, friends, and a nice school; and this one. They have nothing to do with each other. And one of them is over anyway so it doesn't matter. It was a life that belonged to someone else.

"Do you know I am ashamed to bring people over to this house? You are so rude. You are so sullen. You are always with the long face. Sometimes I just want to flush you down the toilet," my mother says to me.

"Why does he have to be here all the time?"

"Because he lives with us and I invited him."

"Well I didn't."

"Don't make me choose, Cathy. I will. And we will both regret it. Don't make me choose."

It never occurs to me that she will choose me.

This is my plan: I will leave my mother and her fuck buddy and move to the Plaza. I don't know why I didn't think of it before. It's perfect. I will continue going to school but I will live alone. I hate them. I hate her. How could she have forgotten my father? There is a candlelight vigil in my heart every day. I promise him that even if no one else acts like he mattered I will. Without going into a lot of detail I tell the Plaza that I want to move in. They don't seem as excited as I am. Plus it turns out to be really expensive. I have money from my father, but not enough to live at the Plaza while I finish eighth grade. And they won't let me check in as a minor. I've got to find an adult to fill out the paperwork. I always thought if you had money you could do anything in this world. But I guess not at the Plaza. I call my brother. He's not a minor. He repeats my plan back to me.

"I got to say, kid, it sounds like not a bad plan. Although quite expensive."

"I know. That's the drawback."

"Well," he says after a long pause. "Let's wait a week and if you still think it's a good idea I'll call them and try to check you in."

"Miss Bunes, the elevator's broken, I gotta take you up in the back," the doorman mumbles to me. I watch him hang a sign up in the lobby that says BE RIGHT BACK. We go to the back elevator. He shuffles his feet. He smokes a cigarette. He takes me upstairs.

"Thank you," I say and go inside. My mother has never been home when I got home from school but someone used to be there—a nanny, the housekeeper, or my sister before she moved out. I do my homework and make some scrambled eggs with dill, and go watch Julia Child. The next afternoon the elevator is broken again. He hangs the sign and I follow him to the service elevator.

"You, uh, want to drive the elevator?" he says after the door closes.

"No thank you." Why he wants me to have a turn driving the elevator is beyond me. What is his problem? I always thought this doorman was weird. I miss Charlie the doorman from Park Avenue. Charlie had soft brown hair and a lilting voice that sounded like the beginning of a show tune. His face lit up when he saw me like he was really happy to see me. This doorman looks like a hit man and he talks like he's got a bunch of loose teeth in his mouth. He's gross but you can tell he thinks he's really hot shit, which makes him grosser.

"Come here," he mumbles. "I'll show you how it works. Hold on to here. Come."

I touch the lever. "Okay. I'm done. Thank you," I say. I think we are finished.

"No. Come closer. Sit up here and I'll show you," he says.

"That's all right," I assure him. "I don't need to drive the elevator."

"Come over here." He pats a space between his legs on the seat he's sitting on. "Sit over here." I shuffle over and sit between his legs on the little metal elevator stool and he takes my hand and puts it on the lever. "There," he whispers sliding my hand and the lever across his lap. He lets go of my hand and holds on to my hips sliding me up and down. I run out of the elevator when we get to my floor.

The next week the elevator is broken two more times. It is never broken on any other doorman's shift or in the mornings. Oh well. This is my new after-school activity, I guess, riding my doorman's crotch. I follow him to the back. He never talks anymore, he just holds my hips and slides me up and down very slowly while I stare straight ahead counting the floors to my apartment, where I go inside and space out until my mother comes home and the sun goes down, putting this day out of its misery.

"What is it that you would like me to do?" my mother replies in a voice I don't expect.

"I don't know. Something," I suggest feebly. "I mean don't you think it's weird that the elevator is broken all the time and I have to go up the back with him?"

"Well, what do you think I should do?"

"I don't know, Mom." I really don't know what she should do. "But don't you think you should do something?"

"Well, I could write a letter," she says finally.

"Okay," I say, assuming the conversation is over.

"But he'll probably lose his benefits."

"Okay."

"Is that what you want?"

"I don't know. I guess so." I just want to go in my room and rock.

"He'll get fired."

"Okay."

"And he will lose all his benefits, Cathy."

"Okay."

"Well, no, Cathy. It's not okay. He probably has a wife and kids and they need those benefits."

"What do you mean? What are you talking about?"

"Their *benefits*. They're probably all covered under his benefits. Their *life insurance*. Their *health insurance*. Their *dental insurance*. Is that what you want? It's a very serious matter. Do you *want* them to lose all those things?"

"I don't know. I just don't want to ride up in the elevator with him anymore."

"I don't understand what you are doing with him in the elevator in the first place," she says.

"The elevator's always broken."

"Well it's not broken now, I just came up in it."

"It was broken this afternoon."

"Well it's not broken now," she says as though the problem is solved. She's making me feel bad. But if I tell her she will say, "No one *makes* anyone anything, Cathy. You can't *make* a person do or say or *feel* anything. I don't make you do anything, whatever you do you do yourself."

"What *is* it Cathy?"

"I don't know," I say, whining.

"I don't know what you want me to do. Do you want me to write a letter? I will. He will lose his benefits. But I will do it. Is that what you want?"

"No. I guess not," I say. It's only nine floors.

My mother has found herself.

After eleven years of being the female traveling companion to a male executive, she has re-entered the work force. Through a connection to NYU and the benefit of several grants, she runs an office operating out of a third-floor space above the Bleecker Street Cinema called the Alternate Media Center. She carries a porta-pack everywhere and is always talking about two-way video interactive this and telecommunications that. It is a very exciting time in her life. She is having a renaissance. Not me. I am in the Dark Ages. She works constantly and the more she works the happier she is. When she goes away on business trips a designated adult stays with me at night and during the day I am on my own. She leaves me with two twenty-dollar bills for my expenses.

"I expect the change," she says.

"Here," I say when she comes back.

"What is this?" she says.

"The change," I say.

"The change? I don't want the change, where are the receipts? What did you spend the money on?"

"The bus, a sandwich. What are you talking about?" I say like she is crazy.

"I want to see what you spent the money on," she says. "I want an accounting." I roll my eyes; she catches me. I am still a child and she is the adult and for some insane reason she is in charge. There is nothing I can do about it. I am supposed to do what she says. The next time she goes away I take a piece of paper and write down what I spend the money on: $2.99 on Clairol Herbal Essence Shampoo, $3 on ham sandwich with mustard and mayonnaise on roll, $3 on bus tokens, 49¢ on blue ballpoint pen. When she comes home I give it to her.

"What is this?"

"It's what I spent the money on," I say.

"This is not what I asked for. Where are the receipts? This is not an accounting. This is a list. I don't want a list. I want to see what you did with the money. I want an accounting with the receipts and a tallying up of what you spent against what you were given." I stand there, dumbfounded.

"Honestly, Cathy. Use your head."

BUXTON

In the middle of eighth grade I suggest boarding school. A friend of my brother and sister's who wrote a hit song for Carly Simon suggests his alma mater. And even though everyone more than slightly suspects him of stealing every single one of my mother's flower and bug pins at a Christmas party three years ago to buy drugs, his suggestion is accepted. The school is small. They call it a community. Kids help build the buildings and make yogurt. You are only allowed to go home four designated weekends a year. Thanksgiving is spent at school. Parents can come visit you. There are no rules, just customs. Every senior makes a speech at graduation. I am given a collection of last year's graduation speeches to take home with me at my interview. My mother is impressed with how self-assured the students seem. I'm not. The speeches are all the same: *Before I came to Buxton I was selfish and now I'm not.* Or subtitled, *I Was Lost and Now I Am Found.* All that impressed me was their policy about leaving. You can't.

I didn't bring the right clothes. My roommates laugh at me every time I walk through the door. I figured the dress code was L.L.Bean, Levi's, turtlenecks, flannel shirts, work boots—in other words, basic country, but it's not. It's charge a bunch of cowl-neck sweaters and gauchos at Bloomingdale's with your parents' credit card and complain when the ice and salt ruin your new high-heeled boots. I dream every night that my mother is burning up in a white clapboard house. I want to rescue her, to save her, but I leave the house empty-handed every time, shaking with fear as red and gold flames leap up and devour it. I stand on the dark street, flanked by the Rocky Mountains, sobbing. Then, as if someone flipped all the lights on at once, the sky turns white. I am blinded by the light and there was no fire at all. Strangers walk past me not understanding why I made such a big deal over a house that wasn't even burning.

I am not allowed to go home for another eight weeks. In the meantime my mother sends me an extra blanket because I am freezing. The box arrives bent and one side is ripped open. The blanket is black and gummy from where it was pressed into the floor of the mail truck and God knows what else. There is no note.

There is a list posted every Tuesday right before they ring the bell for dinner. If the faculty thinks you are emotionally well adjusted there is a gold star next to your name, which means you can study in your room during day- and nighttime study halls. This is not a reward. This is not a popularity contest. This is a custom. I wait by the bulletin board, like a starving animal, ravenous for affirmation. Even though I always have a star I still feel like nothing.

The school wants me to see a psychiatrist. I prepare myself for what my mother will say because I've heard it my whole life: "You know what my mother always said to me? She said, 'Where is it written you have to be happy. Show me where that is written.' You know what a real problem is, Cathy? Cancer. That is a real problem. Stu Weiner has cancer. That is a real problem." But she surprises me. "Well," she says. "I have *real* problems, Cathy, I have to get a new secretary."

There are a lot more customs than they let on about: Don't drink or get high. Don't go in the opposite sex's dorm. Be happy and well adjusted. It is easy to be happy about all the customs because if you are not happy about the customs it means you do not have enough school spirit, which means you are a menace to the community. Which means you won't get a star next to your name and you might have to be removed from the school community, in the middle of the night if necessary, like my last roommate, Theresa, or be held back a year in broad daylight, like Oscar. Oscar's mother committed suicide when he was five and his father is a very busy Broadway producer. They live in the Dakota. John Lennon and Yoko Ono are his neighbors, but he hardly gets to see them anymore because he is away at school. Oscar has been a sophomore twice and is on his way to being a junior for the second time in a row. Oscar hardly ever has a star next to his name.

Another custom is that it is not against the customs to smoke cigarettes. This is a good custom.

A taxi picks me up Thursday afternoons and drives me to my psychiatrist's red barn house. It feels like a house where a family eats dinner together and laughs so much peas and carrots come out of their noses. It looks like a house people can't wait to come home to. I wish I lived in this house. "So why don't we begin with your childhood," she says warmly.

I talk for forty-five minutes. When I'm done she says, "Do you have a mother?"

"Do I have a mother?" I laugh out loud.

"Oh," she says, "because you didn't mention her once." Our time is up.

My first weekend home my mother makes my favorite meal: shrimp ragout with green noodles. My sister, who is back from Colorado, is there and so are some of my mother's friends. My mother says, "Well, Catherine, I think you are in terrific shape. I think that school is fabulous for you. Doesn't Cathy seem like she is in great shape? Here's to Buxton." Everyone toasts me. I am beaming.

My sister follows me to the bathroom. As I pee she says, "I just had a fight with Mom." My adrenaline is pumping. My mother has always liked my sister better. She is the one consulted on family matters, the one my mother talks to, the one my mother acknowledges as an equal. She is the one holding the map in the front seat, like an adult at fifteen, navigating our way across long car trips through France. I am the four-year-old sitting in the backseat bored out of my mind pretending to be a cat. Maybe my sister will finally move over in my mother's mind and there will be room for me. "I told her she was going to lose you if she didn't start giving you credit," my sister continues. "It is so typical of her to give Buxton all the credit for how great you are." She rips off a wad of toilet paper and hands it to me.

"But is that what she meant?" I ask, wiping myself. As usual everything has a deeper meaning to my sister and it went right over my head.

"*Of course* it is," she explains as she pees before letting me flush. "She never gets it. She has no boundaries. I told her, she better start paying attention or you will run away so far, so fast, she will never find you." None of this ever occurred to me. But two days later, as I sit with my head pressed against the bus window on my way back

to school, it is all I think about. I watch the black pavement accumu-
late into miles. The rhythmic pounding of the road under the wheels
lulls me to sleep. I am gently traveling farther and farther away.

Almost half my life has passed without a father. The implications
of this idea get bigger and bigger while my actual memories get
smaller and smaller, until they just turn to dust and disperse in the
atmosphere. I remember nothing that is not captured and secured
firmly in place by a camera. I have a picture of my father and me
fishing in Aspen that my sister took. We carry fishing poles and are
wearing windbreakers. He has wading boots that go all the way up
to his thighs. I don't remember anything else about that day. Everything beyond the white borders of photographs is gone.

    I am so desperate for memories, pictures I'm not even in be-
come events in my life: my parents on a yacht traveling the Greek
islands, the two of them in a restaurant in Europe smiling patiently
as a waiter prepares something tableside. What my father smelled
like, what his voice sounded like, what his hands felt like on my
back—it is all gone. I walk through my life numb, barely feeling
what is happening because it will all disappear anyway. I believe it
is manipulative to miss him. He died a long time ago. It isn't important anymore. I don't tell anyone what I am feeling. I am fine.
One Saturday night I see *Interiors* at the local movie theater. It is
the best movie I have ever seen. It is everything I am inside. I start
pretending I am being filmed. During filming I am not alone,
which is good and I feel good because I am serving a purpose for
the human race. I love the characters in depressing movies. I want
to repay the favor.

I have a dream that I am alone. Everyone is gone and I am walking
through an empty city. The psychiatrist interprets it as being about

my father. She is so literal. It annoys me. I interrupt her and say, "Oh please spare me all the psychobabble mumbo jumbo. My father's death had absolutely no effect on me." I skip my next appointment.

I can devour *Anna Karenina*, *Emma*, *Howards End*, and *War and Peace* but I can't find Czechoslovakia on a map. I remember concepts; ideas but not specifics. The SAT is my new enemy. I score badly enough to seem dumb but not badly enough for anyone to realize that I am just a person who tests badly. Multiple-choice test taking is a skill I don't have. People much dumber than me score beautifully. I manage to get 300 more points than the 250 points they give you just for knowing how to fill in your name and social security number. A tutor is hired so I can get into a good college. At this point, getting into any college seems unlikely. I literally do not get into SUNY. I don't think there is a single New York State resident with a pen who doesn't get into SUNY. I go to a different high school every Saturday to retake the SAT until I get a decent score. The first time I say to myself, "This is the most important test of your life." I score a combined eleven hundred. The next time I say, "This is the least important test of your life." I score eleven hundred. The third time I try a more moderate approach: "This is a little bit important but not that important." I score eleven hundred. The fourth time I go in high as a kite and make a design out of my answers. I still score eleven hundred.

I am the only one to graduate this so-called community with no college to go to. I throw all caution to the wind and don't write the senior speech that everyone else is writing about how lost and selfish they were until they came to this school. My speech is called "This Year's Armor," and it is about how I am no longer going to dress myself in armor and be so tough all the time. It's not true but I wish it were. It is about my mother. I do not want to be my mother. But I'm sure it's too late. I already am her. I don't get a star next to my name ever again.

"I don't understand what the problem is," my mother says.

"Do you really want to know?" I ask, knowing better. The plywood walls of the makeshift phone booth in the girl's dorm are covered in scratches and messages and threats and phone numbers.

"Yes, I do," she says.

"The psychiatrist thinks I have low self-esteem."

"*Low self-esteem.* I don't understand."

"Well, I don't think much of myself."

"That's ridiculous. You are bright and attractive. I don't understand. What's the *matter* with you?"

"She thinks it might have something to do with the summer you sent me away to live with Michael and Leslie because Daddy died and you couldn't deal with me and I overheard them saying they didn't want me either."

"That's ridiculous. You know why nobody wanted you, don't you?"

"Actually, no."

"Well I'll tell you. Nobody wanted you because you were a pain in the ass."

"That's what I'm talking about."

"What?"

"You were always telling me I was a pain in the ass. It made me feel like . . . I was a pain in the ass."

"You were. You were an absolute pain in the ass."

I hang up and let some other girl call her mother.

After graduation my sister and I use part of our inheritance and go to the Bahamas. We sneak into corporate breakfasts because they are free and the pineapple is delicious. We eat dinner in the Howard Johnson's because it is cheap. We order fried clams because we assume they are fresh. The last night of our vacation my sister reads all the fun facts on the sugar packets. Fun Fact #114 is: "Did you know all our clams are flash-frozen and flown in daily from our warehouse in Queens?" When I get back to New York my mother says she can call her friend and get me into Barnard.

"Who's your friend?" I say.

"The president," she answers.

I write an essay about how I had neglected to realize the importance of a women's institution. Not a word of it is true. But I get in.

THE FINGER

I choose premed as my college major. But after my first multiple-choice bio test (which reminds me a lot of the SAT) I realize I will never get into a medical school that is not in the Czech Republic because I don't test well so I might as well have the career that I want as a weeping actress. My mother will be ashamed of me either way. I take an acting class and don't tell anyone. The teacher says I am excellent. He says I am the only one in class who breathes like the character. People pretend to know what he is talking about but they don't. I do. I want to use my life to breathe life into other people. I don't want to breathe my own life.

My homework situation has lightened up considerably since dropping premed so I hang out with my sister every weekend doing massive amounts of cocaine. She works at *Saturday Night Live.* Everyone there does it. We stay up every weekend until dawn doing lines and talking about my mother. We pretty much blame her for everything. It's so fun. We talk about how she never let us mourn for our fathers so we blame her for never getting over it. We confirm that she never has room for all of us in her heart at the same time so one of us is always out on her ass. Except my brother, who is a boy. He is always in favor because my mother feels the sorriest for him.

"It's a man's world, Cathy. Don't you ever forget it, Cathy," my sister says, rubbing her finger along her top gum.

"His father died, when he was six you know, boohoo," I say sticking the straw deep into my nose.

We laugh and pretend to scream in her face. "Yes, we know! OUR FATHERS DIED TOO!" More lines. Then role-playing.

I am my mother. "Well I think it's very hard for a boy to lose his father."

Then my sister is my mother and adds, "And the *women* in this family are just much *stronger*." We laugh so hard we have tears pouring down our faces. We talk about how she always told my sister she was slow and me that I was a pain in the ass and now we have no choice but to wear those descriptions like dog tags around our necks. *Nothing* is our fault. We are simply a product of our up-bringing! More lines. We agree that we will never amount to anything in her eyes if we are not widowed with children before the age of twenty-eight. And then we pretend to feel sad because my sister is thirty-one and already blew it. But it's okay, we console each other, we can just do more lines. I go to every taping and the party after. I see Elvis Costello throw his guitar down on stage and change songs in the middle of the live show and throw everyone into a panic. Me and Gilda Radner throw up side by side in the bathroom at Gallagher's. It is the best time of my life.

I want to be my sister. I try on all her clothes and pretend I live in her apartment. We do more and more and more and more lines. We have a blast. But when the drug wears off it is unbearable. I wish I could sleep; I wish I were dead. But I am wide awake, my skin is crawling and my loneliness has turned my heart into a scab the size of a baseball glove. I feel severed. My torso is lying useless on the couch that used to belong to my parents. My legs are some-where in the bathroom. My sister and I are forging an alliance out of hatred. And the closer we get the farther out my mother gets tossed. "This is wrong," I say. "Can't we all just find a way to live together?" But then we burst out laughing. I need more drugs.

I have lost thirteen pounds. My mother hasn't said anything. At night I see my boyfriend. I wear short shorts and high heels. I take the Seventh Avenue IRT from Cathedral Parkway and change at Times Square for the RR. I get off at Union Square and change for the L and walk to Avenue C. The later the better. My boyfriend is impressed with my street smarts. He should be. I am not afraid. I am too angry for any motherfucker to fuck with me. I defy them to fuck with me. I want them to fuck with me. This is my recurring fantasy: I will take the subway to my mother's house and get in the bath in my old room and slit my wrists and die in the warm water and have her find me. But I am afraid it will hurt. What a pussy. What a fraud. I am never having children. What if they hate me a fraction of this?

I throw up all day. Vomiting causes the release of endorphins in the bloodstream. A surge of endorphins causes euphoria. No won-der I do it so often. Between self-imposed euphoria and cocaine I am okay. I arrive in a taxi across town one night clutching my $120 in cash, only to discover that I am cut off from my dealer. I plead with her. She says my sister doesn't want me to buy anymore. I say, don't *you* want me to buy anymore? I'm a really good customer, aren't I? Yes, she says, you are. So sell me some, I say. She does. My sister reaches a bargain with the dealer: no more grams. From now on I have to buy half ounces. My sister thinks this will make it harder for me. But it doesn't. I use my social security checks. They come on Fridays. My bathroom is covered with vomit. I'm sure it is a metaphor.

My mother agrees to come to therapy. I am dreading it, and I can't wait. The truth will come out. That she never notices me. That I am a burden she doesn't want to carry. That I had a chance to be light and happy and instead I am dark and miserable and should be flushed down the toilet along with my dinner. I have lost twenty-three and a half pounds. "Hey you!" I want to yell. "Your daughter is painfully thin. Did it occur to you that maybe it is because of something you did? Something you neglected?" I walk in the office and my mother is already there. She looks terrified. Her arms are crossed. I kiss her hello and she actually flinches. It is the saddest thing in the world. My psychiatrist says to my mother, "Thank you for coming." My mother scrutinizes me and my carefully chosen ensemble. "Is that *my* sweater?" is all she says.

My oldest sister, Carly, is home for Christmas. While I am snorting up in my mother's bathroom she tells me, "As long as you are throwing up and doing drugs I don't feel comfortable engaging with you." Leslie agrees. I look at them and see that they are fat. My brother, who is home too, takes me into my mother's bathroom a couple of hours later and says, "Kid, they think you are headed for serious trouble." I wait for the part about how he is worried but he says, "I told them you are a relatively smart girl and you'll either figure it out . . . or you won't." And he leaves. I stare out the window at Washington Square Park and am thoroughly dissatisfied with my family. I go in the kitchen and slice myself a cucumber and start eating it with a pair of chopsticks and my mother, who has been glaring at me, says, "Are you going to throw that up?" I look at her with such disbelief and hatred and say, "No. Comments like that make me throw up. Not cucumbers." And I go in her bathroom and throw up.

My friends at Barnard stop talking to me. They taught me how to vomit, they taught me how to dress, they drew up the plans for my renovation. They reinvented me. I am nothing without them

It seems like a good time to transfer. I decide to apply to the drama department at NYU. I know it is what I was meant to do. I can cry on a dime and I have impeccable comic timing. I tell my mother, now a department head at NYU, how much money she would save if I transfer. "Sure," she says. "I could get you in." Until she put it like that I assumed I was good enough to get in myself.

Dr. Mellman thinks I am a danger to myself. She tells me to go home and pack a bag and meet her back at her office so she can bring me to a facility that can help me. I call my sisters, whom I haven't spoken to for months. Neither of them is home. I don't call my brother because I am mad at him. He comes to New York periodically and doesn't call me. Some people, he said, think blood is thicker than water but he doesn't. Just because I am his sister, he said, doesn't necessarily mean he is interested in me. What an asshole. But I wish I were more interesting. I look at my clothes. I have nothing to wear at a mental hospital. I call my mother. What a shock: she is out of the country. I don't want to be locked up. No one will know where I am. I close the door to my room and don't come out for three days. I stop doing cocaine but I never go back to Dr. Mellman. Fuck her.

I take an apartment downtown so I can be closer to NYU and farther away from my bullshit friends at Barnard. I am in a van, driving the rest of my stuff from West 108th Street to Thirteenth Street. I see cop cars lined up in front of my new building. "What's going on?" I ask a person on the street. "Someone got robbed, I think," they say. Wouldn't that be funny if it was my apartment, I joke to the man with a van as we carry the last of my belongings up the stairs. When I open the front door to my new apartment I see that my stereo is gone, my TV is gone, every garbage bag filled with my stuff is sliced open. The contents of my life are strewn all over the floor of my new living room. I pick everything up and try to make a home. It is a cute apartment. I guess I just have to keep the gate locked on the fire escape, and step over the junkies in the front hall, and not light the oven when I am alone so all the mice that fly out from the broiler don't run over my feet.

I am sure I will feel better when my roommate comes. Her boyfriend, Chuck, moves in with us. Chuck is news to me. I don't like running into Chuck and his shlong in the morning. We get a kitten for the mice and to keep me company. Chuck rolls over on it one night and kills it under the weight of his left arm. We fight about money. Chuck thinks we should split everything two ways, even though, as I point out, there are actually three of us. The halls stink like pee and Chuck never makes the rent because he is always lending money to one of the guys on the stoop I have to step over. I complain to my mother. She says, "I'll call the housing department tomorrow. I'm sure I can get you a staff apartment." As usual, I am nothing without her and because of her.

I can't eat anywhere if the bathroom doesn't have a single stall and if the sink isn't close enough to the toilet because I need warm water and I need the water running to help me throw up. I eat, vomit, and go jogging. I've given up cleaning the bathroom. Today there was blood in the toilet along with everything else. It scared the shit out of me. My aggression and despair were aimed at my mother and myself. I never wanted to hurt my internal organs. I call my mother.

"I found a place to help me."

"Well good," she says. Her voice is flat as a pancake.

"They have a session that starts next month. I have to give them a deposit to hold my place."

"How much is it?"

"Six hundred dollars." She doesn't say anything. "It is supposed to be really good." She still doesn't say anything. "Will you pay for it?" I ask finally. She sighs. "What is it?" I ask. She still hasn't said yes or no.

"I don't want to give you the money. Why will it be different this time? When will you get over it? I have been paying for your goddamn psychiatrists for six years and none of them have done you any good."

"That's not true."

"What have they done? You are still bulimic, you still lie, you are still angry. When will you get over it? What are you going to do with your life?"

"There is blood coming out of my stomach and it frightens me," I say.

There is a protracted sigh, and finally, "I'm giving you the money but I don't believe you. It is part of your disease, I read about it. You are in denial and you lie."

The program is a success even though the woman who runs it is chubby and addicted to cocaine the whole time and gets her license suspended six months later. I make one friend. She is in worse shape than me. She shits all over her apartment and cuts herself and finally commits herself to Columbia Presbyterian.

It was surprisingly easy for me to stop. I told them I would stop throwing up if I could lose weight while I digested. I am on Weight Watchers. I am a happy little digester. My mother is glad.

Dinner at my mother's apartment. Alex and Molly are there. I hate Alex and Molly because every dinner I think I am having alone with my mother is ruined when she opens the door and says, "Alex and Molly are here." My mother adores them. They are Canadian and, as my mother is so fond of pointing out, "Alex is a genius." "So what," I tell her. "He's pretentious and a phony."

"He is not. He's just very, very, *very*, bright. He won a MacArthur, you know."

We are in the living room nibbling on my mother's typical pre-meal fare, olives and a variety of cheeses from Balducci's. My mother always forgets to put out bread for the cheese and never provides a dish for the olive pits. Her hostessing style is both gracious and awkward. "Tell us again, Goldie," Molly coos, rolling an olive pit around in the palm of her hand. "Tell us again." They always make my mother tell this story. I don't blame them. It's a good story.

"Well, I skipped grades when I was a kid because I had scarlet fever," my mother faithfully begins. "I was quarantined, and all I did for those three years was *read*. I read books and I discovered that there were places in the world other than Ottawa and people in the world other than my sister and I couldn't wait to see them. I knew one day I would get out, but in the meantime I read and finished high school early. My mother told me I couldn't just *hang* around the house every day. So for the first year after high school I went to the library every day and read. Which suited me fine because I couldn't stand my sister and I wanted to get out anyway.

"And then, when I was seventeen I went to a party at the National Film Board and met a man who took me up in a back elevator to drink liquor. And it changed my life. I will never forget it. I smelled the silver nitrate on the film stock and I was intoxicated. I could think of nothing else. I knew I wanted to make films.

"So I went back the next day. 'Can I help you?' a woman behind a desk asked me. 'Yes,' I said. 'I'd like a job.' 'What can you do? Are you a writer?' she said. 'Are you a director? An editor?' she asked. 'No,' I said. 'What can you do?' she asked. 'Nothing. But I can learn,' I said. 'No,' she said, 'that's not how it works.' 'Well this is where I want to work,' I told her. 'That may be true,' she said to me, 'but unless you know how to do something we can't hire you.' 'Oh,' I said and I went and sat down in the waiting room.

"'Excuse me? What are you doing?' she asked me. 'Well I'm just going to sit here until something opens up,' I said. 'You can sit there as long as you want, but even if something opens up we're not hiring you until you know how to do something.' 'Well I think I'll just sit here. This is where I want to work.'

"So I sat in the waiting room at the National Film Board of Canada every day for two weeks until they gave me a job. And I followed a man down a long hallway to a door with a sign on it that said NFBC DISTRIBUTION. Now, I had no idea what distribution meant but I went back to the woman at the front and I said, 'Excuse me this isn't what I had in mind.' 'I beg your pardon?' She looked like she was going to kill me. 'Well there's just a lot of desks and filing cabinets in there,' I said. 'It's not very interesting. I want to learn how to make films. That's what I came here for. I don't think I'll learn that in there.'"

And thus began my mother's illustrious career at the National Film Board of Canada, where she escaped her family, made documentaries, met two men with whom she had four children and each of whom left her a widow. The end.

Dinner is served.

I meet a woman named Rita Marie Ross. She is Italian. She has ink-black hair in the style of Louise Brooks and a signature that strongly resembles the logo for Saks Fifth Avenue. Her skin is the color of vanilla ice cream and her lipstick is the color of the inside of a pomegranate. She is the most well-read, educated person I have ever met. She is appalled that I do not have a skin-care line. When I invite her for dinner she sends flowers and a thank-you note. She instructs me on the importance of good manners. She takes me to get a manicure every week right around the corner from where I grew up on Park Avenue. She makes me get a Saks card and commit to a moisturizing program. She teaches me that there is no shame in being a waitress. She says everyone in the world has a job to perform and there is honor and satisfaction in a job well done. She worked at a newspaper. She taught English to Raymond Carver. She published two books. She had a baby when she was nineteen and gave it up for adoption. She has lived more than anyone I know except my own mother. She smokes Camel straights, and when she laughs it rocks the room. She owns art. She is forty-five. I am twenty-five. She is my hero. When I meet my husband, who I don't know is going to be my husband, she smiles at me and says in her low smoker's drawl, "Oh, Catherine, you are having a life-changing experience." She is a waitress where I work. My mother doesn't like her at all.

"Sterling Jackson made my knees into jelly," my mother says walking out the double door of her office building. It is a story I have loved hearing ever since I started dating. "I was absolutely helpless. He treated me rotten and I would say, 'I'm not gonna see him anymore,' and the weekend would come and he would call and I would send the kids to my mother's so I could be alone with him. Half the time he'd cancel and I would curse him and swear not to see him anymore and the next weekend would come and he would call and I would drop everything. Finally, thank God, he stopped calling me. Years later I was having a business lunch at the Dorset and someone said, 'Isn't that Sterling Jackson?' And I hadn't thought about Sterling Jackson for years. He hadn't entered my mind. And there I was at lunch and I heard his name and my knees turned to jelly and I thought I was going to fall right under the table. 'Whatever happened to Sterling Jackson?' I managed to ask. 'He just got married,' someone said. 'Again,' someone else said and the rest of lunch was a blur. He made me crazy."

"And then you ran into him again eventually. Right?" I say, knowing the ending.

"That's right. Years later I went back to Toronto for a conference and he was there. I'd heard he'd had some trouble and he looked old. He came up to me and, I'll never forget it, he said in the same voice, 'God I've missed you. Let's get together. Where you staying?' And I said, 'The Sutton Place. Room 217.' But I was staying at the Park Plaza. And the next morning he found me and he was furious and he said, 'Where were you last night?' and I said, 'I must have forgotten,' and I walked away. And that is the last time I saw Sterling Jackson."

My new boyfriend, who Rita smiled so wisely about, is older than me and makes dinner reservations. He wears real shoes. I have never gone out with anyone who didn't wear Converse All Stars or combat boots. He has a car. He has a gold American Express card. He takes me in like a stray. I decide to break up with him because I am bored. But before I do, he appears carrying a breakfast tray covered in red roses. I watch him bring it to me in my bed and have the strangest sensation. I feel feverish and my stomach hurts. And then I realize: I am safe. He makes me feel safe. I borrow money from a family friend to buy him a gold watch for Christmas. I get it engraved "Boy oh Boy." He gives me a gold watch on a chain engraved with my initials. It is very "Gift of the Magi." When he tells me he loves me, I wish he hadn't. It is too soon and I have nowhere else to go. He owns a store across the street from the bar I work in and he watches me every day from his window. He proposes on our one-year anniversary. I call my mother from a phone booth in upstate New York, ashamed. My giant engagement ring doesn't suit me. I feel like I am wearing a big SOLD sign. "I'm getting married," I say. I want to hear her say, "Don't worry."

"Well good luck," she says. And hangs up.

I get a job at Barneys. I can sneak out and run a half a block down Seventeenth Street to the theater I work at for fittings. I can go to rehearsals on my lunch break and my husband can't see me through the window anymore. The dressing room at the theater company is just one room with a curtain hanging down the middle. My husband says this is wrong. He thinks all we do at the theater is undress in front of each other. He says he will start undressing at his store. I tell him it's not really the same thing. "Why?" he says. "If there's nothing wrong with it at the theater then there shouldn't be anything wrong with it where I work. Barneys," he continues, "has separate locker rooms. Why? *Maybe because it is not normal to undress in front of people that you work with!*" He is really bugging me. I get a part in the Issues Project. This year's "issue" is censorship.

"Oh great," my husband says. "Censorship. So what, there'll be like what? A bunch of naked people on stage?"

"Gross," I say. "What is wrong with you? Only someone as narrow-minded as you would think of such a dumb expression of censorship. There are a lot more interesting and imaginative, less literal, classier ways of expressing censorship than taking your clothes off. And believe me, they will think of them, even if you can't."

I storm out. The night of dress rehearsal I watch all the plays for the first time. The lights dim for the first set change and four people silently appear on stage to move the furniture. And what do you know? They are all naked. The naked people come back between every play. There are eight plays. Eight times four, I calculate in my nervous head. That's thirty-two appearances by naked people each show.

I am in so much trouble.

Barneys is the most beautiful store in the world. We have 8:30 a.m. breakfast meetings every other Saturday and I don't even mind. The Hermès meeting made me cry. The same family is still running the business. We ate croissants and watched a video of a sunny warehouse in France where women hand rolled and hand stitched hems on all the beautiful scarves. It showed how every bag is started and finished by the same person who lovingly began cutting and dying it. Every single detail is done by hand. I worship my mother's purses in a new light. Barneys is still run by the Pressman family too. In my orientation they told us how Barney Pressman hocked his wife's engagement ring to open the store. We learn that Gene Pressman, Barney's grandson, is the good-looking fashion genius responsible for opening the women's store. All the girls in my department flirt with him. He throws a lot of parties. He is married to a former model who wears jodhpurs and looks sad all the time. Mrs. Pressman, Gene's mother, always says, "Hello, dear" to me and it is my dream that she will pluck me like a flower from behind the counter and say, "You, little shop girl, you are different than the rest. Come with me."

We get a 45 percent employee discount twice a year for complete outfits. The rest of the time we get 35 percent and it doesn't include accessories. I have three pairs of Clergerie shoes and two Gaultier suits and three Hermès scarves. The display department is the only area of the store run by someone outside the family. The person in charge is a very little man with enormous ideas. He controls everything; the way we fold scarves, the palette of the sock display, the composition of the jewelry display. Cases of merchandise arrive and we have to page the display department so they can oversee the way we arrange it. No one would dare just open a box. He orchestrates the windows along Seventh Avenue and Seventeenth Street, which are very provocative and rapidly becoming important in the retail world. In the fall the windows are going to be decorated with live performance art. I am asked to be in one. I am totally excited. It is my first paying acting job since the TV movie I did in Canada when I was still in college—the one I thought would change my life and give me a career but actually did nothing of the sort. I tell my mother. The event is from six to nine. When I come home there is a message on my machine from her. "I saw you! I saw you in the window. It was fabulous. You were wonderful. You were funny and that hat you were wearing was so dramatic and that dance you did was sensational. I loved that dance. When did you learn to dance? I was so proud I thought I would bust. You were so funny and terrific. You are such a good dancer. Congratulations." I press delete. I wasn't in that window. That wasn't me.

My husband gives me one ten-dollar bill a day. I give him all my paychecks. I do not have a cash card for our account. When I say I would like my own money he says, "Don't I buy you everything you need?" His voice sounds like his heart is breaking. "Yes," I say, "but I have to ask permission. It's my money too. Doesn't that seem a little fucked up?" He also safety-pins my shirts closed so no one can see in the gap between my buttons when I lean over a display case. He agrees to couples therapy after coming home one night and finding me holding the front door knob in one hand and a suitcase in the other. The first day of therapy the therapist says, "People come to couples therapy to break up or to stay together. Why are you here?" He asks me first. I lie.

I can't stop thinking about the fifty thousand dollars my in-laws spent on our wedding versus the money my mother did not contribute. She said she would give us a down payment for a house but she had absolutely no interest in wasting money on a wedding. I felt like Debra Winger in *Terms of Endearment*. His family lives on Long Island. My mother is a snob. She hates Long Island. She has nothing in common with his parents. They are married and they don't read *The New Yorker* and the angriest his mother ever gets at his father is to say, "Ooh, I am going to hit you with a wet noodle." His mother is the nicest person I have ever met. She is warmth personified, softness in motion. She says yes to everyone. She can't prioritize. Everything is equally important for her. Someone's car broke down, someone was just diagnosed with cancer, someone needs a paper clip—she'll be right over. Every time his father sees me he says, "Oh I could pick her up and put her in my pocket." It is purely by rote but I blush and want to crawl into his pocket every time he says it. After we tell them we are separating he never says it again.

Against advice from agents who won't sign me and acting teachers who don't get me, I cut off all my hair and do not get blond highlights. I book a commercial the following week. When the check comes I steal it so I can bankroll my escape. My husband packs my things. He decides what is fair dispensation of our wedding presents (nothing from his parents or any of their friends). He says I may leave, but I must leave behind the boxes he packed. If I still want a separation two months later I can take everything. I move in with my mother. She seems sad. I assumed she'd be happy I took my life in my own hands. That is all I have ever seen her do.

I watch Matthew Broderick win a Tony Award and dedicate it to his father, who is dead. I vow to do the same. I change my name to Catherine Lloyd because when I join the unions there already is a Catherine Burns. Lloyd was my father's first name. I don't want to have the same last name as the rest of my family anymore. I didn't take my husband's name either. I am attached to no one.

"Hello, Miss Bunes." I feel a breath go through me, which is what my acting teacher at NYU always said should happen before you speak in a scene, but I am not in a scene. I am in the lobby of my mother's building. I manage to get myself upstairs.

"Oh Cathy. You are a grown woman. When will you get over it?" my mother says when she finds me pacing the floor like a caged animal. If I had a grenade I would throw it at her. "He's a harmless old man now." She is breaking the rules. She is saying things that cannot be said if we are to share the same life. I will not stay in this apartment another second. But the decision to leave is not empowering. Because I don't know how to stay anywhere.

I have done five commercials, eleven plays, and two television shows, and I still have to work at Barneys. Every morning I walk across Greenwich Avenue and have a conversation with myself *Cathy, you can do it. It's just eight hours. You can do it. You need money and they are paying you for your time. It is a totally fair exchange.* I believe myself until I walk in the employee entrance, punch in, and am instantly overwhelmed by nausea. I can't handle it anymore. My roommate the well-paid working actress came down the marble staircase yesterday all aglow from her ten-thousand-dollar shopping spree. I try to look at it as a challenge to be a good employee. *Today I will fold all the scarves and use the brush to clean out the display case. If I really concentrate time will go by faster. It is easier to work hard than be bored,* I tell myself. But I haven't done it yet. Instead I stare into space and ignore the customers I am not in the mood to deal with. Every morning before we open I call my mother. We are getting along better since I stopped throwing up, plus I got her a really cool Prada raincoat that folds up into nothing. My discount makes me very popular.

"Aren't you at work?" she says. "I doubt calling me on the telephone is what they are paying you for."

"You know what, Mom? Don't worry about them. They're not losing any money, okay?" When I have auditions or a tech at the theater I still say I am going to the bathroom and punch out. But yesterday I left to go to the bathroom four times and really got on the subway and went to auditions. I am starting to feel guilty—even though I am probably saving them money because I rarely work a full eight-hour day. My new boyfriend writes speeches at the EPA for money. This is his work ethic: he hangs his coat on the back of his chair in the morning and rides his bike back home where he writes plays and takes a nap until the end of the day when he goes back to the EPA to say good night and pick up his coat. I tell him it is dishonorable. "I doubt that's what they are paying you for," I tell him. He tells me, "What do you care? I turn in all my work, I write the goddamn speeches. And they're good." I can't tell if he reminds me more of my mother or of me. I am completely in love with him.

The speechwriter wrote an amazing play for me. I play a rookie cop who is overcompensating for everything, for being a rookie, for being a girl. I am proving myself right, left, and center. I love the police force and am grateful to belong to something bigger than myself. I am in love with my partner. His father and his uncles are all cops. He takes me under his wing. I would do anything for him. He teaches me something moral and honorable every day. I will make him love me. I will be worthy of him. In the play I am waiting for him in the lobby of an apartment building while he picks something up. The doorman is trying to flirt with me, which is insulting. I keep calling him a doorman and he keeps explaining to me that he is a security guard. By the end of the play my partner breaks my heart. He is upstairs fucking a whore. And I break my own heart because I am falling in love with the doorman, who is charming and a better person than my partner will ever be, but I can't let myself because I am still a kid trying too hard.

The play also happens to be hilarious. I'm pretty good in it. I win a little award for it. A lot of people from Barneys come. My mother comes and she says, "Maybe you should be a cop instead."

"I beg your pardon?"

"We're going to Paris," my mother repeats out of nowhere.

"We are? What are you talking about?"

"I'm taking us to Paris. I want to show you Paris. I want to take you to Paris. Isn't that a good idea? I just decided it just now. Isn't it terrific? I love the whole idea."

"My God."

"Won't that be nice? For our birthdays. Ach, I can't wait. I am booking the tickets now," and she hangs up. I had been planning a trip to Paris for a week, in September, by myself as recompense for turning thirty and being divorced and once again not being voted into the theater company that everyone I know, including my boyfriend the speechwriter, is in. And I have just been informed by my mother that I am in fact going to Paris for five days, in the spring, with her.

On the plane I read travel books looking for flea markets, trying not to dwell on why, for the sixth year in a row, that fucking theater company won't let me in and my mother reads *Vanity Fair*, which she pretends is beneath her.

"It's for the *plane*," she says.

"Whatever." The seat belt sign is turned off. Our first beverage arrives. "What time is it anyway?" I ask her. I'm thirty, with a divorce under my belt, but I don't have a watch.

"It's a quarter to five, which means it's a quarter to one in Paris except I don't know if they have daylight saving time in Paris. I know they do in London, but the French are so peculiar. What would you like to see first? Where shall I take you first? I absolutely cannot wait to show you my Paris."

"Well, you know," I say, "I was sort of thinking maybe we wouldn't, you know, do everything together. Like maybe—"

"Don't say 'like.'"

"Well maybe I thought we could have adventures, separately, during the day and, you know, like meet for dinner and tell each other everything that happened." And I can see for the first time in a long time, I have hurt my mother's feelings. She hurts mine all the time, but for some reason that's different. I cannot bear hurting hers. I want to be my Jewish person's idea of Catholic and repent, so I take it back: "But we don't have to do it that way," I say. "I just thought you liked doing it that way."

"Why would I want to do it that way?" she says.

"Because you did it that way with Spencer last year and you said you had such a good time."

"Don't be ridiculous. That was *Spencer*. He's *impossible*. And we hate whatever the other one likes. He wants to drag me to those hideous flea markets, he likes to go to very expensive restaurants. He's awful. This is totally different. You're my kid. I'm taking you to Paris. It's my gift to you. I want to share it with you." I had not thought of it like that.

In Paris, we reach a compromise. I am allowed to visit the hideous flea markets and she is allowed to undermine my sense of self. We eat steak frites every night we are there. Eating so much steak frites makes her very rude to the waiters. It is as though she is embarrassed at how much steak frites she eats so when they take her order she just wants them to go away. "Steak frites!" she barks at them.

I, on the other hand, try to order very sweetly. We drink a lot of red wine and people watch. She kicks me under the table whenever there are Germans nearby because she is a Jew who grew up during the Holocaust and can't help it. I would never tolerate this in New York, or anywhere in America for that matter, but somehow in Europe it seems different. I let it slide.

"What's the matter? Are you all right? Are you not enjoying yourself? What's wrong?" she says staring into me. Nothing is wrong. It is quite the opposite. Everything is great. Sometimes my mother has the uncanny ability to read my thoughts and totally reverse them.

We visit Chartres. On the train my mother says, "Look at all the ticky-tacky houses."

"Yeah, I was just thinking that."

"Do you remember that song?"

"What song?"

"The ticky-tacky houses song? It was a song on a Pete Seeger record you used to like to listen to when you were little." I don't remember actually, but I remember her telling me I liked it so many times it is as though I remember. Past the outskirts of the city we travel through fields and meadows where the grass looks so soft I want to take all my clothes off and lie down in it. We roll through little towns where it seems as if every blossom is blooming and every bud is bursting. There is euphoria in the air, as if all of nature is jumping up and down saying, "The leaves are coming! The leaves are coming!" I point out the buds and blossoms to my mother. "Mmm. They are so delicate," she says. There is a long pause. "And things of delicacy don't last."

We walk through the town of Chartres eating amazing sandwiches: tuna fish, hard-boiled eggs, cornichons, and tomatoes on bread that is so delicious it makes the contents irrelevant. We inhale and savor every bite. Halfway down the block my mother wants to turn around and get another sandwich. "No!" I say. "If you do you'll be too full for steak frites later." She stops cold.

We arrive at the church. I get very emotional and respectful in churches. My mother doesn't, which I don't entirely understand, but I can tell she thinks her reaction is infinitely more practical than mine. In the back and up some stairs, a grail, some swords, several priests' robes, and an entire outfit worn by Charles V are on display. I am moved to tears. I can tell my mother wishes I wasn't. I can't get over how old everything is and how long it lasts. It both comforts and depresses me. The exhibit is behind Plexiglas and an old plainclothes nun is sitting in front taking collections. I give her a heap of money. My mother shakes her head. As we walk out she says, "I think it's the balance and the proportion. You know." There is a long pause for me to visualize the balance and the proportion. She continues. "Yes, that's what it is. The balance and the proportion. The height and the space. You know? That is what makes good architecture."

The last night we go to Île Saint-Louis to hear a concert in a church. She tells me the first time she saw Paris was at the age of thirty-two. She took a different lover each night she was there. She doesn't say how many nights she was there but she does tell me that the first time she saw the ocean was at the age of thirty. The music starts. It is Bach's *St. Matthew Passion*.

"*He's* very good," she says hitting me in the shoulder. "He must be Jesus." I know exactly what she means. No one can sing that beautifully and not be Jesus. At intermission my mother gets up to stretch her legs. She comes back and hits me in the arm.

"Well don't you know," she says. "The pushy German in all the furs managed to get a seat in the front row." That the pushy German might have had a ticket entitling her to sit in the front row never crosses my mother's mind. The German is German. And my mother is, after all, my mother.

LOS ANGELES

The theater company that I am not a member of decides to do the cop play in L.A. so I am in L.A. I can barely keep my eyes on the road there are so many things I have either read about or seen in movies or listened to in songs: Sunset Boulevard, La Brea Avenue, Rodeo Drive, Beverly Hills, the Hollywood sign, Santa Monica, palm trees. It is thrilling and crazy. I am staying with an old friend from Barneys who relocated and lives in the cutest apartment in Beverly Hills and her zip code is literally 90210. When the play closes I have two things I didn't have in New York: an agent and hope. But I need seven thousand dollars. I call my mother.

"So, does this mean you are not coming to the Hamptons this summer? I rented another house you have managed not to see."

"I can't. My agents really want me to stay to build on the momentum. I'm testing for a show next week."

"I'd rather send you to France to chef school. Would you rather do that? You are thirty-two. How much longer are you going to keep doing this?"

"I have to stay. It is so like me to come out here and then leave before anything good can come out of it. I always leave."

"Okay. Call Leigh and she'll transfer the money. You deserve it," she says. "Everyone deserves one last chance." *She always comes through*, I think. *And then makes me feel like shit.*

I leave the speechwriter and make a permanent home for myself in L.A. I leave everyone. I leave them and then like a baby try to crawl back to my mother. Because she is alone. Because she is the only noble person I know. Because I love her more than I know how to love anyone else, including myself. My heart is shattered. Shards of it are on my lap, on the ground, spread everywhere. I love the speechwriter. I love him and I don't know how.

My parking spot says, RESERVED FOR CATHERINE LLOYD BURNS. My dressing room says CATHERINE LLOYD BURNS, the call sheets say CATHERINE LLOYD BURNS, my paychecks, my contracts, my scripts and rewrites, which get delivered every night, say it. The name Catherine Lloyd Burns literally falls at my feet each morning when I open my back door and the script delivered the previous night lands inside. My father's name, Lloyd Burns, is alive and looming large. It is beautiful. I feel like I have his blessing to be an actress.

The pilot gets picked up and I start making seventy-five hundred dollars a week for thirteen weeks. It is less than half of what everyone else on the show makes. But it is more money than I ever dreamed of being paid. My ex-husband helps me make a budget. He has become my family away from home. I don't make a move without talking to him first. It is the strangest thing how close we have become. In him I see a kind of generosity I have not known from anyone. I suddenly understand why I married him. He is wonderful. But mostly he let me leave. He let me leave and fought to keep my friendship when I was gone. No one has ever been as kind to me in my life.

I write down every dollar I spend in a notebook—his suggestion. I pay my mother back. I get rid of the '84 Volvo that I crashed twice and bought used, against his advice. I lease a new car that he approves of in both safety and monthly payment. I fly first-class all over the place and go to network events and think of my father as I smile and pose with countless network affiliates. I have a brand-new life. My mother calls me one morning and wakes me up.

"Did I wake you?" she says.

"Yes," I say. "That's okay."

"No, go back to sleep. I can never get the goddamn time difference sorted out. Is it three hours earlier or behind?"

"Earlier, it is six in the morning."

"Oh my Jesus. I don't know how I am going to remember that, you would think I could remember. Oh I woke you. Go back to sleep. Hey your picture is in the paper," she says.

"Really? What paper?" I ask.

"*The New York Times.*"

"Why?"

"With a review of your show. I'm afraid it's not very good. It is an awful review. They hate it. But the picture is sensational." And she hangs up. I have never lived anywhere but New York. Now I am three thousand miles away. It is unbelievable how liberating distance is. Distance and money.

While I'm visiting New York on a hiatus, my mother buys me an Hermès scarf. I love it. She has the same one.

"*God,*" my sister says, "she suddenly approves of you because you are making money." There is acid in her voice.

"That's not true. We had a really nice couple of days together. It's just better now because we don't see each other as much." I agree with myself. But my sister never will. She is always the expert.

"You don't get it, Cathy, you never have. We are either inter-changeable or one of us is on her shit list. Remember when I worked at *Saturday Night Live* and she was so impressed because I had status and money and we had the same fucking Missoni sheets?"

"I loved those sheets. I always wished I had them."

"Now she doesn't approve of my life so I don't get the scarf. It is always on her terms. You live in a fantasy world with her. You al-ways have. You think you have a relationship with her but you don't. One of us has to be outside. This is your time. I'm out, you're in. It's been that way from the beginning. She can only love one of us at a time. One of us is always in the doghouse."

I hang up furious. My sister always discounts whatever I am able to enjoy about my mother. I lie down exhausted and gaze at my new scarf.

It looks defiled.

My mother comes to a taping of my show. She actually tells me about thirty-five times that she is proud of me. It is like an out-of-body experience. We hold hands the whole time she is in L.A. I keep wishing my father were here. Walking around the Beverly Center the next day before we see *Fargo*, she says, "I have to buy some wrapping paper, can we stop in here?"

"Sure," I say, leading us into Papyrus.

"I'm so proud of you. Can I buy you a present?"

"No thank you."

"Ah, come on. Let me buy you something, please."

"Mom, I don't need anything."

"Ah, I never see you anymore. I want to buy you something."

"There's nothing I need in here. But thank you."

"Look around. Maybe you can find something," she says. So I look around and find some little glass disks you put on your can-dlesticks so the wax doesn't drip on them. I hand her four.

"What the hell are these?" she asks. I explain them to her. "Why don't you just clean the wax off yourself? Why do you need this?" she says.

"I don't. You said you wanted to buy me something."

"Well here. Give them to me. Are you sure this is what you want?" The lady behind the counter rings her up and my mother is incredulous. "Twelve dollars and sixty-four cents. Twelve dollars?! Twelve dollars? What the hell costs twelve dollars? Let me see the receipt." My mother and the cashier analyze the receipt while a long line of shoppers wait impatiently. "Oh," my mother says exasperated. "It's the candle things." Distance and money, distance and money I keep repeating to myself. It is my new mantra.

There is a new item in my mother's front hall. It is a giant, extremely blurry, black-and-white photograph of a woman's ass. I don't care for it. No one does. "Face it," my brother said when he walked in the front door, "you've been taken by the ass." Beverly Roth, an art dealer and my mother's new friend, is responsible for the ass. My mother seems happy that none of us get it. "You may not like it, but that does not mean it is not art," she says blithely. I say, "Why do you like it?" She does not answer this question.

Beverly owns an important gallery in Soho. My mother adores the world she moves in. They went to the Venice Biennale last year. They rent houses together in the Hamptons. They go to the Golden Door at Christmas to avoid us. Beverly comes to all family events now. Sometimes her children come too. Beverly is alone like my mother, successful, and smart as a whip like my mother. One of her clients had a show of Nautilus machines covered in frozen Vaseline. The catalogue is prominently on display in the center of my mother's coffee table. The art in the living room, which used to be a shrine to my parents and their travels, is replaced by art Beverly tells her to buy: a small black box containing an electric LCD device is constantly flashing red provocative messages near color photographs of a man tied in ribbons wearing a goat suit.

I am in my dressing room.

"I'm going to Italy with Beverly," my mother informs me on the phone.

"Italy?"

"Italy. Ever since the Biennale. That's where I want to be. I can't explain it, I just know it in my gut. The country is so exquisite. The terrain, the people, the churches, the olive oil. I could just die it is so magnificent. I don't want to be anywhere else. I've decided to rent a house there for the summers. I'll get a house and a snappy little car, maybe even a red car, and I'll drive around, and be in Italy with my new friends the Italians. Hopefully my children will come and visit, but if they don't then they don't. Acchh, I'm so excited." And she hangs up.

I am on location in Austin. I have a part in a movie with John Travolta. People in Austin recognize me from my TV show. I like it. But the windows in my room don't open and I am overlooking the atrium, which is a forest of fake plants and bar stools. I can't wait to get back to my apartment in L.A. It is the nicest apartment I have ever rented and the only apartment my mother hasn't cosigned for. It is mine. Every month I write out the rent check and am newly amazed; I can afford it.

"I think you are so terrific. I don't think I tell you that enough. You are terrific. And I love you," my mother says to me on the phone out of the blue.

"Wow. What brought that on?"

"I don't know. It's almost your birthday and I was thinking about you and I realized I probably don't tell you the good things enough. I want to get you something really special for your birthday. What do you think you would like?"

"Well you know that thing called e-mail and the Internet?"

"Would you like a computer?"

"I think it's time I joined this century. Even though I fear they will ruin the fine art of letter writing.

"Consider it done."

"Thanks, Mom. But you don't have to buy it for me, that's not what I meant. I can afford it, you know. They pay me pretty well. You could just advise me."

"Don't be ridiculous," she says. Two weeks later a laptop arrives at my dressing room on the Paramount lot. Six months after that, on another hiatus, I come to New York. My mother takes me around her office and her department, proudly introducing me to her staff and her students, not as the daughter who is a regular on a prime-time series on NBC, but as the "daughter she just bought the eleven-hundred-dollar Mac for."

Derrick puts me through. I try and stop him, but there is no stopping him.

"I was in a meeting when you called before," my mother says.

"Yes, I know."

"Who answered the phone?"

"Amber."

"Ach, I have told her a hundred times she's supposed to, they are all supposed to, everyone who works for me is instructed that if any of my kids call—"

"Yes yes yes to put us through."

"Yes. To put you through. But she didn't. I don't know what's the matter with her. Everyone in this office knows that if *any* one of my children calls they are to be put through immediately. You know that too."

"Yes, we all know that policy, but it is extremely annoying to interrupt you in the middle of a meeting unless it is urgent, which in this case it wasn't, and you can't talk anyway—you're in a meeting. I hate when they put me through. I don't want them to put me through."

"Well they are supposed to. Thank God Derrick knows what he's doing. Is he the one who answered this time?"

"Yes."

"So what is it Cathy? I'm in a meeting. Some people have to work for a living. I'll have to call you back." And she hangs up.

"I'm buying a house in the Hamptons," she tells me. "That's it. I just decided."

"What about Italy?" I say, thumbing through the rewrites that just appeared under my dressing room door.

"I'm done traveling for the time doing. It's ridiculous. Guess how much it cost me to fill up the car in Todi? Eighty dollars. It's ridiculous. You have no idea what is happening to the dollar."

"How will you afford a house in the Hamptons?" I ask.

"I have no idea," she says.

"How will you get around?"

"I'm buying a car. I guess. I don't know. I just decided. So I don't know. But I'm done with traveling. It's too much and it's too expensive. It is totally ludicrous. So I decided I'll get a house for all of us and I'll go when I feel like it and it will be close enough for you guys to use and that's what I'm going to do and we can spend Christmas there. I have this fantasy that my family will all come to be with me at the same time. I have no idea how I'm going to afford it. I don't care. I'm going to spend it while I got it. That's my new thing. I don't want it when I'm dead. So I'm going to spend it while I got it. I might as well live it up now."

"I'm getting married," I say. She groans and says, "To the one from New Jersey?"

"His name is Adam."

Adam has white hair like my ex-husband. We play gin like I did with my father. We drive the same car except his is white and mine is black. I hope that this is not a metaphor.

"Ughh, it's going to be like *Long Island* all over again, Cathy." And she hangs up.

"Hi, Mom."

"Hello," she says. There is about as much warmth in her voice as in twelve inches of tightly packed snow. I'm back in the doghouse. What was my infraction? I wonder. Forming independence? Getting engaged? Who knows.

"What's new?" I say, forging ahead.

"Nothing is new, Cathy. I am trying to run a department." I am too old to have her disapprove of me, to be punished for what she considers bad choices. I know that. And yet that is precisely what is happening. "How's the new house?" I make myself ask.

"It's a lot of work, Cathy." Her tone implies that I will never grasp the hardships of living in the real world—let alone how demanding having a house with a swimming pool and a rose garden in Bridgehampton is. "Everyone is coming in August," she says. "Barb's been a terrific help. She moved into the guesthouse and has been helping me with everything. It is really a lot of work."

So Barb's back in. Excellent.

"Well I guess I'll see you and it in a few weeks," I say.

"What do you mean? Are you coming?"

"What do you mean, what do I mean? I'm coming when Michael and the girls are coming."

"You are?"

"Yes," I say. "That was always the plan."

"I didn't know that," my mother declares.

"That was always the plan. It's been the plan since Thanksgiving."

"I didn't know that. You're coming up from Los Angeles?"

"Yes. Where else would I be coming from? What is going on?" I say.

"Nothing is going on, Cathy."

"You're being weird. Are you mad at me?" I ask.

"No, I am not mad at you, I simply was not aware of your plan."

"My plan? We've been talking about it since before Christmas. I haven't seen the house or you or Michael or Barb or the girls in almost a year."

"Well I was not aware. I remember you saying something about that, but I suppose I didn't bother to register it because you change your mind all the time."

"I changed my plan because Rita committed suicide. You're still mad because I went to Rita's funeral instead of coming to see you at Thanksgiving?"

"I don't know where you are planning on staying," she says.

"What are you talking about?"

"I didn't know you were coming. I don't know where you are going to sleep."

"What are you talking about?"

"I am talking about the fact that it is a very small house and all the rooms are taken."

"All the rooms are taken?" I repeat. Freon courses through my veins.

"Yes, all the rooms are taken. It is a very small house."

"So there is no room for me?"

"I am afraid not," she says, and I hang up, shivering. The balmy eighty-degree Los Angeles weather cannot possibly warm my skin. I forgot how horrible the doghouse is. I know I have lived in it before and survived, but I can't remember how. Every time I am put out, I am unprepared. I am not going to the Hamptons. Fuck her new house. Fuck her. Fuck my sister who played her cards right and is now my mother's current favorite.

I make a plan. I will not come home. Ever. I will stay in California and I will make enough money to buy a relationship with my own mother. I will take us back to Paris. I will send her a new Hermès scarf every now and then. I will make her proud of me but I will not come home. In my plan I will learn not to care.

Adam's brother throws us an engagement party in New York. We aren't staying with my mother. I always stay with her. But now I have options. "I don't like your lobby," I tell her. "Oh, Cathy, when will you get over it?" she says.

"Dear Mom," I fax.

I wish I could explain to you that if you ever want to say anything regarding the incident with the doorman the only appropriate thing to say is: "I'm sorry that happened to you." Telling me he is harmless is just insane, insensitive, inaccurate, and irrelevant. So is the fact that he has aged. None of this has anything to do with what happened. What happened is, he took me up in the elevator and he jerked off against me. Saying: "When will you get over it; it was a long time ago" or "He's a pathetic old man" is in fact a negation of what happened and what it was like for me. You don't know what it was like. I survived and I have sex and I travel and I function and I have a job and an apartment and friends. You do not need to fear that I am emotionally crippled. But if you ever think that I like to see that man—that I like knowing he still works in your building and has maintained his benefits for the last twenty-five years—you are off your rocker. His face makes me sick.

You did not take my side then and it is something I have worked very hard to reconcile within myself because I do not want anger at the past and at you to rule my life. I think I have done quite a good job. I am proud of my relationship with you; frankly I cherish it. But it is really too much to bear when you continue with the comments I have described. Please, in the future say nothing at all or, "I'm sorry that happened to you." And if this doesn't make sense to you I wish you would talk to a psychiatrist about it. I do not mean this in a mean way. I promise. I will see you soon. With Adam. Oh my God. Love Cathy.

I call her ten minutes later breathless. She takes my call immediately and it always amazes me, the courage she has regarding me. She says, "I got it. I got it." I don't know if she means the letter or the contents of the letter. But it is good enough for me.

A few months later I am sitting in my sun-drenched dining room admiring the bookshelves I just had built. I have had boxes and boxes and boxes of books—labeled from Auster to Wharton—stacked in my garage for two and a half years. The handsome gay designer who drew the plans was horrified that I actually intended to fill the shelves with books. "Oh dear, no. Objects," he said. "Objects."

"No. Really books," I insisted.

With my books filling the shelves and surrounding the room on all sides I feel like I live in a real home. I always wanted a room filled with books.

"I'm coming to see you for the weekend," my mother says, calling from New York. I haven't had a real conversation with her for months.

"You are?"

"Yes, in two weeks. Beverly invited me to see one of her clients at the MOCA and the opening of another client's movie. I thought it would be so much fun to see you." If my sister were here, she would tell me that my mother isn't coming to see me. My mother is actually coming to see Beverly. I am just the waste product excreted after digesting the real nutrition of her trip: Beverly.

"Great," I say. "I'm so excited. Do you want to stay here?"

"No. I don't want to put you out," my mother says.

"You won't. You haven't even seen my apartment yet. I can sleep on the couch and you can sleep in my bed."

"I don't want to put you out."

"You won't. It would make me so happy to have coffee with you in the morning and to pass you in the hall on the way to the bathroom."

"Okay. Great!" my mother says. But I can tell she would rather be in a hotel.

The first show on Beverly's list is an installation by Robert Gober. A white room suffused with light echoes with the sound of running water cascading down a white staircase. The space is empty except for a serene statue of the Virgin Mary, punctured by an enormous lead pipe. She is flanked by two identical suitcases lying open on either side. They are leather, handmade, old-fashioned, and substantial. The kind of craftsmanship that went into them is exactly what is missing in this world of the Duane Reade superstore and the ugly giant cement multiplex. The statue is beautiful: calm, benevolent, and maternal, and sublimely indifferent to the fact that she is impaled. Aside from my bookshelves, it is the most beautiful thing I have ever seen in my life.

The suitcases, on closer examination, are bottomless, revealing a gurgling subterranean stream under the museum's floor. The stream is home to gently moving plants, black and opalescent mussel shells, giant copper pennies, and little luminescent fish. The effect is magical and the care that went into making each object is mind-blowing. Gazing down, at a certain angle, you can see the naked legs of a perfectly cast man with skin that is almost transparent. He is holding a baby. Is the man saving the baby? Is he going to drown the baby? Everything is so beautiful and haunting; disjointed and injured; and yet it gives me hope. My tragic little Jewish self is not alone. The Virgin Mary is with me and all our mutual sadness will go down the drain in the center of this floor together, illuminating something beautiful forming beneath the surface. I am so grateful to my mother for knowing Beverly Roth; I never would have seen this show otherwise.

We go through the rest of the museum and I see a solid white canvas that turns my aesthetic rapture to rage.

"What the fuck is that?" I ask my mother.

"I don't know," she says. "I really don't profess to know enough about the world of contemporary art to know what it is."

"So just take a wild guess," I say.

"I guess it is a response to what constitutes art. It is a challenge," my mother says.

"Hasn't that been done already? Like a lot?"

"I don't know enough to comment," she says and walks away from me and my loose lips.

We move on to a pedestal supporting a black garbage bag stuffed to the gills.

"Nice. What's that?" I ask.

"I don't know, Cathy. I told you I don't know enough about

contemporary art to have an opinion." My mother, the former trailblazer, has become a docile lamb. I guess Beverly wears the pants in their relationship.

"Okay. But what does your gut say? Do you like it?"

"Cathy, I am not in a position to have an opinion."

"Come on. You are the most opinionated person I know."

"I'm changing," she says.

"You are?"

"Yes, I am."

"Well I'm not," I say. "And I don't care for the black garbage bag. It is not as bad as the mess made out of the cardboard boxes over there, but it is no Robert Gober."

"Cathy," she says sternly, "you may not like it, but that does not mean it is not art." She continues to move away from me and my uninformed opinions.

Behind the garbage bag hang two small sheets of white paper. Not surprisingly titled *Two Sheets of White Paper*. The black garbage bag artist is responsible.

"What do you think of this one?" I ask.

"I told you I am not knowledgeable enough to have an opinion. I don't know what I think." I am so disappointed, I barely recognize her. I can't let it go.

"When has your education, or knowledge on a subject for that matter, prevented you from having an opinion?" I say. "You never went to college, you are a professor at a major university, you run a department at the same university, you are on boards all over the country. But according to the new you, you're not qualified to do any of these things. You've never done anything the way anyone else does and that's what makes you so admirable." We leave the museum in silence.

At dinner Beverly is pleased to hear we like the Gober piece. I ask her about the two white pieces of paper guy.

"Oh, Tom Friedman. He's wonderful, isn't he? He's quite clever.

Don't you think?" Beverly says, puncturing the flesh of her grilled fish.

"Actually, no. That and the garbage bag did nothing for me," I say, my mouth full of pasta.

A friend of Beverly's takes over.

"What he did was take a sheet of white paper and crumple it in his left hand and then he took another sheet of white paper and tried to re-create the same creases with his right hand. He also did a wonderful piece where he carefully sucked a package of Life-Savers into descending size. It was quite beautiful."

"Oh," I say.

"See," my mother says like a mean girl from seventh grade, securing her position at the popular table. "It really is quite fascinating, *if* you understand the language."

"It is, I agree. I feel much better about *Two Sheets of White Paper*, but I wouldn't have known what he was trying to do if you guys didn't tell me."

"You would have to do your homework," Beverly says curtly. "You have to do some work. Conceptual art is not for lazy people."

"That's right. That's right," my mother says, and she manages to dote on Beverly and castrate me with the same two words.

"Well I think it is for rich, well-connected people. I think art is supposed to reach people, not alienate them."

"The information is available to anyone who wishes to become educated," Beverly says.

"That's right," my mother says.

"How?" I ask.

"Galleries, reviews, art magazines," Beverly rattles off.

"Really? Like if I went into your gallery and said I didn't understand a piece someone would walk around with me and explain it to me?"

"Absolutely," Beverly says.

"Even if I wasn't going to buy it?"

"Absolutely. People always assume we are snotty. We are there to educate, to illuminate. And we will, for people who deserve it. But we have no time for lazy people. We have no patience for people who are not genuinely interested, for people who simply come in to sneer at the prices. People have to do some work. People have to show a little initiative."

"There is no such thing as a free lunch, Cathy," my mother adds.

No one speaks to me for the rest of the evening.

"Cathy, there are some things you know nothing about," my mother says on the way home. I have embarrassed myself in front of her friend. But she embarrassed herself in front of me. She is not who I remember, who I admired. I leave her at my apartment and go spend the night with Adam at his office, which used to be his apartment. She is mad because I chose him over her and I am mad because she chose Beverly over me. It never occurs to me to spend the night with her and live through the discomfort. All I know is that none of the TV shows I am on are important enough to get me out of the bad place with her.

The test is positive. Two pink crosses magically appear on the white stick. I can feel the blood moving through my body. I feel in my body and out of my body at the same time. All my life I have sat on toilets shaking like a leaf, staring at pee-soaked sticks. All my life people have talked about wanting babies and I listened like an outsider. I understood nothing that they were describing. I felt no connection in my heart or my body. I never wanted a baby nor did I feel physically capable of carrying one to term either. I was too short, too thin, too flat-chested, too narrow, too girly. And now I hold the stick; it's positive and I don't have a lick of fear in me. I have no idea why. Maybe I am grown up. I call my mother.

"I'm pregnant."

There is a pause.

"Well, that's what you always wanted."

I hang up. This is not what I always wanted. I never wanted it.

Driving across Robertson Boulevard in my leather-upholstered, climate-controlled Saab 9-3 with its five-CD changer, I understand I have gone soft. I have grown accustomed to the weather (or lack of weather, depending on how you look at it), the disingenuous flora, the wealth, the cancerous show business seeping out of every crevice . . . it's not good. I park at the hideous white cement parking structure outside Ralph's to do some shopping and something snaps. "Where are you from?" is the single most frequently asked question a person has to answer his or her whole life. My poor child will have to say, "L.A. I was born in L.A. My mother was an *actress*, so you know . . ." Whatever horrid things I will be responsible for, at least I can spare my child that. My child will be born in New York. My child will answer the question proudly. I fill my trunk, smiling in spite of myself because even though L.A. is so evil the produce is so good. I am overwhelmed with the need to go home. I suddenly cannot bear being pregnant, harboring a growing person inside my womb, so far away from her. I want my mother. I pull into my driveway possessed by something much stronger than any other desire I can recall. I really don't see how this will end well. But I am going home.

Part Two

IT'S A MAN'S WORLD

I haven't lived in the same city as my mother for six years. My mother's office is at the end of an incredibly long hallway. It is as far back as you can get. She's in a meeting. But as usual I am ushered right in. She gets up. She hugs me. I am so glad to see her, to smell her, to be in her arms. I'm so glad I decided to have the baby here instead of in L.A. We embrace. I whisper so as not to disturb her meeting. "It's so nice to see you. I really missed you."

"Nya nya nya nya," she says back in a mocking singsong voice that makes me feel like I am being made fun of at recess. My eyes sting and well up. A ball forms in my throat. I can't swallow. It's okay, I try to tell myself. It's okay. You're just a grown woman in your mother's arms. It'll be okay. It will be okay. I will be okay.

I am on the F train. I watch a six-year-old sitting next to her mother. They talk, they sing songs. They are completely enchanted with each other. They have their own language, their own rhythm. They are beautiful. I feel the person growing inside me and for the first time long for a daughter. I watch the little girl throw her arms around her mother. This child won't grow into a raging hate-filled teenager who blames her mother for anything and everything she can. This little girl won't spend the rest of her life in therapy trying to figure out what went wrong. Look at them. There is no way that is going to happen. It is so reassuring. The girl's father sits opposite them. He is working. He rifles through his briefcase; he's all business. He glances over at them; they are laughing. He has no time for this. He studies his paperwork and makes a lot of notes. I am in awe of motherhood. I feel energized by the very idea of motherhood. I'm not scared anymore. It's going to be so easy. All you have to do is love the child, pay attention, be respectful. I can do that. I know I can. I feel so ready. They reach their stop. The doors open, the mother's hand reaches out for her daughter's, and the little girl reaches to take her father's hand instead.

In my next life I'm coming back as a man. I will have sex with my wife and come inside her until she gets pregnant and then I will stand up or sit down next to her in the hospital while she figures out how to get it out of her. I will play with my children when I'm in the mood and stop when I don't want to play with them anymore and I won't get all psycho about it. I will throw them up in the air super high and get them wound up right before they're supposed to go to sleep and then I will let my wife, their mother, put them to bed. I will have the best body I've had in years because having children means that I get up so early in the morning I end up going to the gym on a regular basis for the first time in years. I won't worry about it if they don't eat or sleep or move their bowels for days or weeks on end. "Would you stop worrying," I will tell their mother, my wife. "What do you get yourself so worked up for?" And then I will go out. I will enjoy life more than I did before I had children because fatherhood has shown me dimensions of my heart I could never have imagined, and everyone I know will agree, it's made me a much better man. At night I will sleep like a baby because I am a man. I know it is my wife, their mother, my daughters will hate in fourteen years. Not me.

"You look wonderful," my mother says over lunch. "How do you feel?"

"Good. Big."

"The yoga has been fabulous for you, huh? You're just going to breathe that child right out of you."

"I hope so."

"You will. You are in fabulous shape. I only gained eleven pounds with you. How much have you gained?"

"Sixteen."

"Well, you still look terrific. You really do. That kid's going to slide right out of you. You slid right out. I had no drugs. I wanted the drugs, but you just slid right out. You came right out and you were beautiful. You were pink and perfect and there wasn't a mark on you. You were just absolutely perfect. You looked like a little miracle. And I remember I'll never forget your father standing there staring at this perfect little baby. He had never seen anything so beautiful."

I go home and go into labor.

I am holding my baby. She came out of me. I don't even know her yet. But I know she is mine. She is my responsibility. I tell her that many times a day. She lies in my arms wrapped up, her eyes like slits, her tiny fists rolled up tight, and I say gently to this amoeba who barely breathes on her own, "You are my responsibility." It is three o'clock in the morning. She is crying. I have no idea why. She doesn't want to nurse. I'm pretty sure I burped her. Her diaper is dry. What to do? I sing to her. I do not wake my husband. I walk with her. I sing while I walk with her. We make a continuous loop from the living room around the kitchen table and back again. Thirty minutes go by like this and she's still crying, but I am not scared. I don't know how to make her stop crying, but I know she is not alone. I feel completely at peace. I can listen and not solve anything. I can just be here. I can be a lap, a bosom, a woman who is patient. I am somebody's mother. I am just here until the crying stops.

Olive is three days old. I am changing her diaper and she is screaming her head off. My mother sneaks up from behind and says, "Ach, I just love that sound."

I don't like that people talk about babies like they aren't people. It's true some babies seem like they are still swimming around in the fluid, like they're not all the way here yet, but not Olive. She's very alert. She's kind of intense, actually. She always looks like she is trying to figure something out—my face, her arm, a snap on her onesie. She is clearly intelligent. She fits in the diamond of my cross-legged legs. She rests her head on my knee and pushes her little feet against my thigh. She sits there all day long and I marvel at her, gazing at her face, touching her fuzzy head, picking at her cradle cap, playing with her fingers, massaging her little bod, totally in awe of her. I tell her everything: who's here, where we are, what we're gonna do next, and when I'm not talking to her in my lap or on my shoulder, she's in the sling. "We intend to keep her in the sling as much as possible," my husband and I told our parents last night. "Are you sure that's good for her?" they asked, terrified. "You're breaking her neck!" my mother screamed on her way out the door.

"Are we? Breaking her neck? Does she even have a neck?" I ask my husband as soon as we close the door behind them.

"It's fine. She's fine. They don't know what they're talking about. We're doing the sling. They did it their way. It's gonna be fine," he says. Then, "I don't know. Let me try to get her in there again. Where's the directions?" I hand him the sheet of paper that came with the sling. He reads it and fiddles with Olive and says, "Give me the page with the picture on it, will you? I want to make sure I know what I'm doing." Meet the parents.

"Olive, aren't you tired? Shouldn't you go to sleep?"

"Cathy, it's almost two in the morning. Come on," Adam says, rubbing his eyes.

"I know. What should we do?"

"Let's just get into bed and pretend we're going to sleep and then maybe she'll fall asleep."

"Genius, Adam. Okay little wonder, we're all going to bed now. Let's change your diaper and give you some milk and then let's all go to sleep." I change her and nurse her and we put her between us in the bed and turn out the lights and breathe deeply. In and out, our breath goes. The sound of it is completely intoxicating. Relaxing like a massage. I feel totally at peace. I hear my husband drift off for real. His breathing becomes even deeper. I have a new family. It is my family. I love my family. I am with my family. I lie next to both of them listening to the sound of their breathing. I inhale, then double-check to make sure Olive is still alive.

My mother is standing in the doorway, as she has every day since I came home from the hospital, three weeks ago, just to look.

"You can come in," I say, trying to get her all the way inside.

"No. You're nursing."

"Well yeah, but you can come in. I can talk to you."

"No. You should be concentrating."

"All right, but I could use the company."

"No. I just came for a minute. You should concentrate."

"I *am* concentrating. But I can still concentrate if you come in and talk to me. Come in."

"I just came for a minute." And she's gone.

I am eight and something is going on between my parents. I could hide behind the green chair in the living room and listen to them while they go at it, but I don't want to. I have other things to do, like eat my breakfast and leave for school on time. My sister used to take me before she went away to college but now my mother takes me, which means we're late because she's always late for everything. When I'm late for school I have to open the front door by myself, which I can't. It is wrought iron and weighs a ton. I can't even budge it. My only chance of getting to the other side of the door is to sneak in behind a bunch of other kids who weigh enough to get it open. I live in a constant state of panic that I will spend my day in exile, standing on the wrong side of the door, while everyone else is on the other side, the right side, learning things and making playdates.

When the fighting stops my parents make an earth-shattering announcement. From now on I can go to school by myself, without my mother. I take my toasted bagel and my book bag and leave, nice and early, to wait for the Madison Avenue bus. Things couldn't be better. I feel like the star of my own life. I even have a good feeling about the door. As I cross Park Avenue I happen to glance over my shoulder and my mother is walking right behind me. I tell myself that I must be imagining things. The next day I could swear I see her again, on the bus, in big sunglasses with her characteristic Hermès scarf uncharacteristically tied around her head as though she is avoiding the press. I wave at her. She ignores me. The next day I see her again. I can't believe we both have business in the world at the same time. It is too incredible. I see her right behind me crossing Park Avenue. I turn all the way around and I say, "Hi, Mom." She pretends she doesn't hear me. I say it again, she shushes me and shoos me away with her hand. I decide to leave her alone. She must be in a bad mood. We end up sitting across from each other on the bus. I try not to look at her. But this seems crazy. Finally she says, "You're not supposed to see me."

"Oh," I say.

"I'm following you. I've been following you for a week. It's the only condition under which your father will allow you to go to school unescorted. He is so impossible. He thinks you are going to get kidnapped. Your father," she tells the entire bus, "is such a pain in the ass."

Now that the cat's out of the bag I figure we can talk to each other the rest of the way.

"No," she says and goes back to being incognito.

AFFECTION DEFICIT DISORDER

Olive is lying in her bassinet under her mobile. She looks like she's on a psychedelic mind bender. She can laugh at those black and white dangling spirals for a really long time. My mother is visiting. If Olive cries I go over and talk to her. I see what's going on, make an adjustment, then I tell her I'm going to talk to my mother but I'll be right back if she needs me. Everyone thinks it is crazy that I talk to her as though she understands the English language. My mother thinks it's the most ridiculous thing in the world. She tolerates it because I am her daughter and because she thinks I am neurotic, which incidentally, I did not inherit from her and which she pronounces *nyourotic*. Nyourosis is my lot in life because she took a chance and reproduced with a man who was very, very nyourotic. The blame for my condition rests solely on my father's and my father's father's shoulders. Not hers.

Neurotic or no, my infant daughter is not going unattended to, ever, end of story. I can handle my mother's exasperated tolerance, but what really chips away at me is the certainty she has, written all over her face, that I am creating a damaged child. That I am, in fact, damaging a child who would be fine, if not for me. I know what she thinks; my husband's parents think it too: "Babies cry.

That's what they do. It's part of life. They cry. They get over it."
Blah blah blah. They say it to me like I don't know that babies cry.
I know babies cry. Of course they do. When they are upset. So
when my baby cries it is my job to figure out what is upsetting her.
It's her only way of letting me know something's not right. Everything is new to her, the customs, the language, the time difference.
She might as well be on Mars. Since I booked her ticket I better
help her until she knows her way around, until she is settled into
this life. I can't help it. That's what I'm here for.

"What's she doing?" The pediatrician asks at our three-month
checkup. "Is she cooing?"

"Yes," we beam. Right on schedule. What a blessed baby she is.

"What else, is she swiping at things? Making eye contact?
Tracking you across the room, smiling?"

"Oh yes, yes." I'm so impressed with our doctor. I love her. I
offhandedly ask how much sleep babies Olive's age should be getting because all the other babies I know do nothing but sleep and
Olive is always awake and incredibly alert.

"Twelve to sixteen hours a day." She says. "They need a lot of
sleep."

"Oh," I say nonchalantly, even though panic is ringing through
my head like a car alarm.

"How much sleep is she getting?" The doctor asks me.

"She's not getting that much," I answer casually.

"Well, she should sleep ten to twelve hours at night and take
three naps during the day."

"Really," I say. I quickly do the math in my head and realize
Olive only sleeps about nine hours a day. We all sleep from 1:00 or
2:00 a.m. until 9:00 (with Olive nursing every two hours) and then
she nurses one last time and we wake up for real again around
eleven. It was a really good schedule, I thought.

"How much is she sleeping?" the doctor repeats.

"Not that much."

"Is she napping?" Napping? Never.

"Not really. Whenever I put her down she wakes up. So I try to walk around with her while she's sleeping but sometimes it's not possible."

"You have to get her to nap."

"How?"

"Figure it out." I can't believe this is this idiot's advice, "Figure it out." I hate our doctor. If I could figure it out I would.

"You have to do whatever it takes," the doctor says. "Rock her, walk her, put her in the Baby Björn, put her in the swing. Do whatever you have to do. But she needs to take naps. Babies need a lot of sleep. What time does she go to sleep at night?" My husband and I explain, sheepishly, that she goes to sleep when we do at around midnight or that sometimes lately we try to trick her by pretending to go to sleep and turn off all the lights at two or three in the morning if she doesn't seem tired yet. The doctor is outraged that an innocent baby is on this college-student-all-nighter-cramming-for-midterms-going-out-to-see-a-band-family-bed-hippie-dippie-bullshit schedule.

"No," she says sharply. "That is too late for a child to go to sleep. You are going to be in big trouble when it is time for her to go to school. She needs to go to bed by seven every night and she needs to take three naps every day and they need to be uninterrupted and forty-five minutes long. Some people say a nap doesn't count if it's under forty-five minutes but I am willing to allow a half-hour nap. But there have to be three of them. They need a lot of sleep," she repeats.

I'm hysterical on the walk home.

"Adam, what are we going to do?"

"I don't know, Cathy. We'll put her to bed earlier. That's what we'll do," he says like it's no big deal.

"But we're seven hours off schedule!"

"We'll figure it out. Would you calm down? Anyway if she doesn't nap . . . then, whatever." I hate him. This is how *we* will figure it out. *We* won't, and *we* won't worry about it. That's his big plan? He has no plan. He's not worried and he doesn't care. He sleeps through the night anyway. He hasn't got a clue. Obviously I am the only responsible parent in this family. I'm going to have to figure this out by myself. I always have to do everything by myself. I look over at Olive: she is sleeping! I calm down. But the seven-hour bedtime/sleep deficit is still freaking me out. And she sleeps between us, so does that mean we have to go to bed seven hours earlier too? I am hysterical again.

"Adam, what are we going to do?" I ask him again.

"Jesus, Cathy. You're driving me crazy," he says. I look at him and know I will leave him. I have no choice.

"Don't wake her up," I hiss. "And when you tell me how we are going to close the seven-hour gap between what we are doing now and what the doctor says we have to do, then I will calm down."

"What is your problem?" he says like this is the last straw. "You are really out of your mind. Do you know that? I don't know how we'll do it, but we will. Tonight we'll put her to bed a little earlier. And we'll keep doing it until we get her to bed at the right time."

"But how long will that take?" I say.

"I don't know, we'll do it fifteen minutes every few days. So I guess it will take a few weeks. We'll do it gradually."

Gradually? What a horrible plan. He's an idiot. I married an idiot. I had a child with an idiot and even if I leave him she still has half his genes in her. I can't believe I married this man.

Crossing the street I make a startling realization: I've never done anything gradually in my entire life. Of course I married this man. He is the opposite of me. He is the most important person I know.

He is capable of doing things gradually.

"Put her down."

"Yes, Mother," I say, ignoring her. Olive is happy only if I am holding her and walking around. She wants to be touring, seeing the sights, and you have to tell her about them too.

"This is the kitchen. Where cooking happens. But you don't know about that yet. One day, when you eat food, it will interest you."

"She needs time to herself."

"I know, Mother," I say between explanations of kitchen appliances.

"Then put her down. You'll smother her."

"Yes, Mother. Thank you."

"She needs time to be alone. That's when she learns things. Don't you have a playpen? She should be in a playpen."

"She's nine weeks old. She doesn't have a playpen and she's not going to have a playpen. I don't believe in them. They're like little cages." I breeze past her with Olive's well-defined chin—her only real feature thus far—resting on my shoulder. I have to keep moving or she'll start bawling.

"What's wonderful about cribs and playpens is that they pull themselves up. They learn to stand. How is she going to learn to stand?" My mother, tired of shouting after me, has joined our walking tour. She leaves the kitchen and positions herself in the doorway.

"Jesus. On a chair, on the couch, a table, a shelf. She's not *not* going to learn how to walk and stand because she's not relegated to a box for alone time." Olive is crying. "Excuse me, I'm trying to get back into the kitchen. She's sick of the living room."

"She needs to be alone," my mother says to the empty room. When Olive calms down my mother takes her from me.

"What are you doing?"

"I'm putting her down."

"All right. But I don't think that's what she wants."

"Well, we'll see," she says as she places the baby on the floor under a new, Grandma-bought mobile. Olive starts to cry immediately.

"She wants you to pick her up," I say.

"Let's just see if this works."

"If what works? Ignoring her?"

"No, Cathy. My God. This is what I used to do with you. I would try and distract you." She is shaking the mobile in Olive's face. Olive starts screaming.

"Distract me from what?" Suddenly my whole personality makes sense. No wonder I get so enraged when I think people aren't listening to me.

"She just wants you to pick her up," I say.

"Let's see if I can distract her. I did raise three children, you know." She waves a stuffed crocodile in her granddaughter's general direction. Olive continues screaming.

"Distract her from what?" I ask again. "I don't understand. From what she wants? I think she just wants you to pick her up."

But there is no reasoning with my mother the child expert who successfully reared three children by the distraction method.

Finally I say, "How's it going?" My mother looks at me, exhausted from all the distraction. I pick Olive up, she stops crying, and that is the end of that.

Things I am not good at: change, letting go, people leaving me, not taking things personally. So what business do I have having a baby? A baby who grows into a child. Who grows into an adult person who doesn't like you anymore. None. That's what kind of business. I'm doomed. Who am I kidding? I'm not generous enough to love someone just so they can leave me. So they can come home and steal my sweaters, expect me to store stuff for them indefinitely, tell me that the way I do virtually everything is wrong or at best annoying, break my heart with a memoir detailing my personality and its flaws.

Well, it's too late now. The damage is done. And I love this little tiny person so much my heart is running out of my body; it's dripping all over the floor. It is the first time in my life I have ever been completely present. And there is no one in the world capable of more tenderness than her. The way she looks at me. The way she lies with me. The way she caresses me. The way she ever so gently pats various parts of me while she nurses as if she is feeling the parameters of me—surveying the property she owns. A little soft warm hand pats my breast, finds my rib cage, touches my arm, grabs onto the folds of skin that were once my stomach. We belong to each other. And it is the most perfect arrangement I have ever had.

My friend Pam Blaire has a teenage daughter. They were eating lunch together yesterday and Pam was looking at her daughter thinking how spectacularly beautiful she was and how much she loved her and how she was amazed by the miracle of life all over again, by the fact that this person had come out of her. And her daughter, completely grossed out, looked up over her pizza and said, "*God.* Would you stop looking at me that way."

My mother and I are walking down Sixth Avenue. She hits me in the arm and says, "Well have you ever seen a more unattractive group of people in your life?"

"Who do you think you are?" I say. "The queen of Sheba?"

Who am I? My mother? I sound just like her. I squeeze Olive's hand. I hope she doesn't notice.

"I beg your pardon," my mother replies. "I am simply expressing myself. I can express myself." She is appalled. She didn't carry me in her womb for nine months so I could talk like this to her.

She finds my behavior shocking. "I have the right to express my-self," she repeats.

"You are not expressing yourself. You are passing a sweeping judgment. That is not the same thing."

"I am entitled to my opinion. You don't have to agree with it. But I am entitled to it. And I have never seen such an unattractive group of people all gathered together in my life."

Since my mother believes everything in life is a choice, she is totally comfortable blaming unattractive people for their bad looks. It's their choice after all, so if they don't want people like her criticizing them they should choose to look better.

"One day," I say, "one of those people is going to give you a klup on the head. And you know what? You will deserve it. You can think what you like, but you cannot say certain things out loud."

"Why not?"

"Because it makes you one of the rudest, most unattractive peo-ple I have ever seen. That's why."

We don't speak until Olive starts screaming at the corner of Twenty-first Street. It's feeding time. We dive into Barnes & Noble where I commandeer a leather club chair, sit, and try to nurse my baby. It's not so easy. She sucks heartily, but when the milk starts she pulls her mouth off. Now her face is all sticky and she's still hungry and I am soaking wet. I hate it when she does this. The atmosphere has to be just right or she won't nurse. I start gather-ing our things, but before we leave my Jewish mother, who lost her brother in World War II and has a mistrust of all things Ger-man, insists on buying Olive every single Eric Carle board book in the store.

"He's German," I say. I am not looking forward to carrying them all home.

"He must have been born here."

"He was," I say. "But he moved back when he was six. It says right here on the back of the book."

"Cathy, that's enough," my mother says and hands the cashier her platinum American Express card.

Olive and I take our books like good little girls.

I can't let Olive cry it out. Mark and Regina let Owen cry for eleven days and eleven nights. I can't do that. I'm not going to do that. It is just wrong to do that. And yet Owen and his parents are sleeping ten straight hours at night and I look like the drug-using, bulimic, failing Barnard student that I used to be. My clothes are dirty. My hair is dirty. I am too skinny. I am so sleep deprived I am either giddy or crashing so far so fast I get the spins. I might as well be using drugs and not eating. I am eating. But who knew constant breastfeeding and chronic fatigue were better than any diet plan? I am wasting away. But who cares. My baby falls asleep peacefully in my arms and I take three naps a day right beside her even if my nipple proper has to stay in her mouth the whole time. So be it. I am her mother. It's part of the job.

My friend Mary sleep trained her daughter. Mary always looks great. She wears actual clothes. I wear underpants and a T-shirt and maybe, and if it's a special occasion, a pair of slippers. Please tell me what the point of getting dressed is, of doing anything with my hair, when in precisely two hours I am getting back into bed with my baby and my waterlogged areola—where I will stay until her nap is over. Mary's child takes two unassisted ninety-minute naps a day. Mary has time to clean her house. Mary has time to go to yoga. Mary has time to do something with her hair. Mary has a life. Hail Mary.

"Are you ready? One, two, three . . . whee!" I say and let go of the swing. It is so much fun to see Olive sitting up. Let alone sitting up in a swing. We are having so much fun.

"Aaahh!" she gurgles and claps her hands. My hair blows in the wind as we laugh and look into each other's eyes like star-crossed lovers. We are a greeting card. We belong in a slow-motion Clairol commercial or in a tabloid spread of unauthorized photos of TV stars playing happily with their privileged children. I love my life. Then from behind me I hear, "Enjoy it. It goes by so fast." And everything is ruined. I would like to kill the next person who says this to me. I am such a defensive little fucker, and I would like to blame it on exhaustion, but I am pretty sure it is just my personality that causes me to take offense at this remark. These are the thoughts that go through my brain: *They're on to me. I am not really a loving mother. I'm only an impersonator. I am, in fact, only someone fantasizing about being a loving mother in* People *magazine.*

Motherhood isn't very forgiving. You are very judgmental about other people and very tough on yourself. Plus it is lonely. Even though you get a lifetime membership in the Motherhood Club, it doesn't guarantee companionship with anyone you actually want to hang out with. The Motherhood Club is worse than any clique you thought you had managed to escape. Family-bed mothers aren't welcome at the Ferber mother's club. Stay-at-home mothers don't like working mothers with full-time nannies. Attachment parenting, wooden-toy-from-Vermont-no-Disney-crap mothers can't hang out with mothers whose idea of a healthy snack is Doritos before a Happy Meal. Everyone may give everyone the wave on the street but it's a fucking jungle out there. *"Jesus,"* I think, noticing another mother pushing her kid in the swing three down from me. "She looks happy. What's her story?"

Once I asked Mary if she ever felt fed up, if she ever lost her patience when she knew she shouldn't or if she ever felt she was just doing it all wrong. I was ragged and ugly and Mary was all made up and showered and she said, with such concern in her voice, "No. I don't think I have felt that way." Mary had to say that because our relationship will always be guarded. We belong to different clubs.

My husband reminds me that I always tell everyone the truth, which most people don't, even to themselves, let alone the other members of their club. But even I, most honest of all, feel the pressure in the park to be the best Stepford version of myself.

I was wrong. It has nothing to do with how much you love them or how much you pay attention to them. It's all about sleep. Katya put her kid on a schedule by the time he was eight weeks old: structured sleep, structured feedings, structured play. He learned to sleep eight-hour stretches by the time he was ten weeks old. He learned nursing was not a time to fall asleep. She held his feet in ice water to teach him. When it was time in the schedule for sleep she let him cry. I thought she was a barbarian. But the barbarian is so happy and well rested she's already five months pregnant with her second kid. Olive is ten months old now and I am so sleep deprived that I've lost all my confidence. Who cares that I always say "one, two, three" before something's about to happen—before I pick her up, before I turn on the noisy coffee grinder, before I put her in her bath; that I make up songs about what we're doing and sing the day's events to her, that I adore her with all my being. Who cares because it is four-forty-five in the morning and she's awake and I can't get up. I don't want to get up. Instead I watch the red light escalate and decline on my baby monitor like someone in the ICU watching her life-support system. I am in bed paralyzed, flattened by my incompetence and humiliated by the distance between who I am as a mother and the mother I planned to be. I believed loving her would correct everything wrong with the world. It's not true. It has nothing to do with truth. And I have no interest in living in a world where loving someone isn't enough.

Olive slept until 5:00 a.m. without waking up. I slept seven straight hours. In a row, ladies and gentlemen, not seven fragmented, mismatched hours rummaged from the trash of various days and nights, but seven solid hours. I feel like I spent the night at Elizabeth Arden. I look like I had my eyes done. I'm a new person. I have hope. I'm really good-looking. I love myself. Is there light at the end of the treacherous tunnel of sleep deprivation? Is she sleeping longer because I dedicated my life to making her feel safe and attended to and I'm an exceptionally good mother, or just because I gave up and let her cry and I'm a bad mother and she's so depressed that she gave up? Is she sleeping longer because she is eleven months old and it was going to happen anyway and everything I do is irrelevant? Am I boring? My husband certainly thinks so. He says I have a one-track mind. He says I have become the kind of person I previously couldn't stand. That is my fate since becoming someone's mother. I become those I used to criticize.

I never intended to forgive my mother. Forgiveness is so cliché. I spent my whole life seeing her side, mourning her two dead husbands and her youthful double widowhood, reminding myself that her life involved more terror and heartache by the age of twenty-eight than I would know at any age, but I always held on to my moral upper hand. I was the child. She was the adult. And she was supposed to look after me even if her husband died, even if she worked, even if she was unhappy, and even if I was miserable and therefore the last person she wanted to see at the end of the day. Children don't ask to come into this world. And I absolutely believe that it is a parent's job, a parent's responsibility to make their children feel wanted. Parents brought them in. They owe it to them. But here I am. Loosening the grip of my moral upper hand.

I am putting Olive down for her nap. She fits in the crook of my arm and her fat, firm, pink cheeks are resting on my skin. She looks up at me with her big beautiful eyes, which are the exact same eyes I used to have, when my eyelids were still smooth and the whites of my eyes were bright, and she smiles at me. My heart melts. I could die from love. And I wonder if my mother ever loved me like this. How is it possible that love like this gets away when you once held it in the palm of your hand?

"Ba. Dowell. Wuff. Diggy. Daddy. Gaga," Olive says from her crib. I open one eye. It is true. She is wide awake. I have to get up. I fumble out of bed exhausted until I see her little pudgy arms sticking straight up. The instant I see those arms, any part of her, I wake right up. I pick her up, ecstatic. Her personhood is like adrenaline. She is my Red Bull.

"Good morning, little wonder." I kiss her all over. Her breath is warm and smells like steamed milk; pure and sweet and delicious.

"Come here, lovey." We go into the kitchen. "Will you help me do a project? We have to cut up some green peppers for your black beans." I stand her up on a chair and show her how to put the peppers in the Cuisinart. I make the most delicious baby food. I make pureed carrots with fresh dill and sautéed fennel. I make a yellow dal, with garlic, turmeric, and cumin finished with a drizzle of olive oil and a squeeze of lemon. I make a puree of fresh peas and basil. Applesauce with cardamom and cinnamon. I make her cod with sautéed onions, tomatoes, spinach, and potatoes. "Okay. Now push the button."

"Loud," she grins. She is so cute.

"It is loud."

"Againdt," she says.

"Okay push it again."

"Againdt."

"Well, lets put the scallions and the cilantro in, okay?"

"All gone."

"Uh-huh, the peppers are all gone and now we have to put in the cilantro."

"Sonto."

"The cilantro. Okay, push the button." She does. How much pleasure do I get out of a sixteen-month-old not only eating and adoring exceptional food, but also using one of my favorite appliances? A lot. I'm such a JAP. "Okeydokey artichokey, now we have to measure the beans and pour them into the pot. Excellent," I say. "Fantastic pouring, Olive. They all went right in the pot. Here, can you put in the bay leaf, and now can you pour this stuff in the pot too. Excellent."

When the beans are cooked we get dressed and go to the park. Madison comes over with her nanny.

"Hi there, Madison. What'cha got there? Some chalk?"

"Mmhmm," she says to me. "Write my name," she tells her nanny.

"Okay, Madison. What letters do I draw?" Madison spells her name. Oh, for Christ's sake. The alphabet. I should have been teaching Olive the alphabet this morning. And not just this morning. The alphabet's the kind of thing you have to work on for months. Fuck the black beans. I could have opened a goddamn can. My priorities are so screwed up.

I am obsessed with the idea of whether or not we go to the park enough. Owen is in that park from sunup to sundown. He runs his ass off. Olive is, by contrast, a really good pourer. She's incredibly happy, but what about exercise? What if she gets to school and hates recess? I can easily see her faking a stomachache to avoid team sports. I comfort myself with the thought that even though Owen is always in the park, he would probably enjoy some time at home. Kids need both, I tell myself, and then I'm not comforted, because I already successfully established to myself that Olive doesn't go to the park enough.

So as she sits happily with her Montessorri/Martha Stewart–

style egg carton full of hand-cut shapes and textures making a fabulous collage and I make a restaurant-quality meal for our dinner, I panic. We should have gone to the park. We should have gone to the park and eaten pizza like normal people. Oh, well, a normal person would say, and then, being normal, would promptly drop it. It would be over. The normal person would move on. But not me. No siree. It's not over for me. It springs eternal for me. The more I mull it over, the more I shudder. And the more I think I've blown it, the more I can't let it go, and I return to the act of making the decision to stay at home to make dinner instead of going to the park and I retorture myself with all the implications of that decision. Which actually is the beauty of this technique because I get to worry in both directions, backward and forward. I'm a genius.

"I am terrified of cancer," my mother says looking up from her book. "Every year I get a mammogram and I am terrified."

"Breast cancer's probably the best one to get," I say, thinking of the people I know who are still alive with chunks of their breasts removed or entire breasts lopped off.

"No, it's *terrible*," my mother says like she's talking to a complete imbecile.

"I *know* it's terrible, of course it's terrible. But everyone I know who had breast cancer is doing well."

"Well everyone I know is dead."

"If I get cancer I am beginning to think I wouldn't have chemo. The way it poisons you seems more horrible than the cancer."

"I'm afraid if I get cancer I'll do something drastic before I figure out what's really going on," my mother says. And I'm sure that is exactly what will happen. She is so impatient she will swallow her Hemlock Society recipe before she gets all the information. The phone will ring and she won't be able to answer it because she will be dead, which will be unfortunate since it will be the doctor's office calling to say, "Sorry, we made a mistake. It's a cyst. It's benign."

"What about Tilda Bravmann?" I ask. "She didn't have chemo, did she?"

"Tilda Bravmann, I will never forget. They opened her and closed her right back up."

"Because it wasn't worth it?" I ask.

"*No*, not because it wasn't *worth it*," she snaps. "Because there was nothing they could *do*. And I will never forget, they closed her up and the first thing she did was get a face-lift. And then she went to Japan. She traveled the world for cures. And shopping. Cures and shopping. She went everywhere. And she looked sensational."

"And she lasted a while, right?"

"Five years."

"I don't know what I would do since I don't have cancer and I have no idea what it would be like, but I think I'd rather last five years without chemo. Which always devastates your body and your life without necessarily killing your cancer."

"You have no idea what you would do. And you have no idea what it is like to have small children to look after. That changes everything," my mother declares, and goes back to her book. I sit there quietly and wait for Olive to wake up.

We are going to be late for our first music class. Olive's never napped this long in her life. I didn't enter this kind of professional napping into my calculations when I signed up for the one o'clock session. Damn. I've been looking forward to music class for weeks. The first thing that happens in music class is that the purple-haired tattooed teacher and her guitar sing hello to everyone. The kid's faces light up with anticipation and delight at the prospect of hearing their names sung. "Hello, Emma, it's good to see you. Hello, Diego, it's good to see you too . . ." It's corny. But I think Olive will get a kick out of it. Apparently I will get a kick out of it. When she finally wakes up we race out the door. She's still half asleep, and we fly down the street—Olive, her stroller, and I—over curbs, under awnings, through gutters, across intersections. When we arrive they are still singing the song. I am thrilled and start pulling her out of her stroller, but she won't come out. It is so frustrating. They are almost all the way around the circle. Three kids left. I pull harder. But she won't come out. What is wrong with this stupid stroller? My kid is stuck and if I don't get her out, she won't be part of the dumb welcome song. The dumb welcome song, which is almost over. I start really yanking.

"Uh-oh," Olive says.

"Uh-oh is right," I agree, still pulling. "I can't get you out of your stroller."

"Uh-oh," she says. I can feel the other mothers looking in our direction. I try to pretend I look like I know what I'm doing. I look down. It appears I forgot to undo the safety strap and her safety strap is holding her nice and safe like a well-designed safety strap should. She's not coming out until I undo that strap. I am in a hurry and not paying attention. I do everything too fast. I am my mother.

I feel something I have never felt before. I'm pretty sure that it's resentment. I don't approve of resentment. I've said for years, and I've agreed with myself every time I've said it, "I don't approve of resentment. It's your life. Do what you want with it, but don't resent other people for living theirs." But can I just say this is how my husband spent his day yesterday? He got up an hour and a half later than me, wrote for a few hours, went to the gym, ate lunch, took a shower, went to a screening, and then came home, where dinner was waiting for him.

This is how I spent my day. I got up at six-twenty with Olive, nursed her, played with her, fed her some breakfast, played with her some more, tried to take her out grocery shopping, but realized she was too tired, so I put her down for a nap. I went out to buy groceries (taking advantage of my upstairs neighbor's good graces), came home, started to make two pounds of meatballs, realized I was too tired, so *I* tried to take a nap, realized I was never going to fall asleep because I had to make two pounds of meatballs, got up, Olive woke up, I made her a bottle, made the meatballs, made a sauce, took her and her stroller on the subway to meet my mother for lunch, came home, put her down for her second nap, fried the meatballs, packed a care package of food for my friend who just had a baby, played with Olive, delivered the food, went to the shoe repair, went back to visit my friend with the new baby, showed Olive the new baby, wept at the sight of a newborn, wept at the sight of a newborn nursing, wept at the sight of my friend's breasts, full and heavy with milk, darkened by big nipples like bull's-eyes for a little blind baby to find in the dark, came home, and lovingly served dinner to my husband and his friend. He'll argue.

He'll say he set the table.

I want another baby.

"You know you have to empty the can," my mother says. The can she is referring to is a tiny, overpriced Italian garbage can she bought to comfort herself because she spent time in Kmart in the Bridgehampton Commons buying a crib and sheets and other necessities for the room Olive uses when we stay here. The can is insane. It holds two diapers, *tops*.

"Yes, I know," I say. "I've been taking it down every time I change her diaper. It's really annoying."

"Well you can leave *some* in there. For a little while."

"Oh," I say. "I thought you wanted me to empty the can." I sound like my husband. I sound like all men, actually, who habitually repeat back to you in the most literal manner possible your previous statement, attempting to make you feel like an idiot. (Me: "We need to buy Olive winter boots." Man: "No, we can't afford to spend *money* on things that don't matter, Cathy. She'll wear them *once*." Me: "*No*, she'll wear them every day it's *cold* outside. And it's absurd that we can't spare *twenty-five dollars* on *winter boots* for our daughter." Man: "Oh, then I guess I'm too '*absurd*' to have opinions. I guess I'll never express myself again. Obviously I don't *know* enough to have opinions that matter!") It's not a good technique. I'm actually ashamed I've resorted to it, but I feel like rubbing it in that her idiotic garbage can is bugging me and I've run out of ideas of how to do it. I'm sure my mother is as unimpressed with my verbal skills as I am. I call my husband to complain.

"She's driving me crazy," I tell him.

"She's just like you," he says, annoyed. "She just wants to have an argument. It serves you right." Well that certainly made me feel better.

"Look. Look at the hind leg," my mother beams. Olive is moving herself across the floor. It is quite exciting. She stands in a V, feet firmly planted on the ground and hands out in front on the floor ahead of her. Pretty much a perfect downward-facing dog. Then she lifts her right foot, crosses it behind her left foot, and lies down. This leads to a sort of plank pose, which allows her to push herself up again into the V and start the whole series again. It is her own sun salutation. Up and down. Up and down. No one understands how the physics of this works, but between standing up and lying down, she actually moves herself forward two inches.

"Her *hind* leg? What's her front leg doing?" I ask.

"Look at her. I could just watch her for hours. It is like living with a kinesthetic sculpture." My mother, so enchanted (by both her granddaughter and her comparison of her granddaughter to a kinesthetic sculpture) that she says it again. "It is like living with a kinesthetic sculpture. Look. Look at the hand."

"Duggy," Olive says pointing at me. And then, because it makes her so happy, she says it again, "duggy."

"*Nooo.* That's your mama," corrects my mother.

"Daaaddy," Olive beams. My mother looks at me with total exasperation. Olive brings me my slipper.

"Dooggy." She brings me the other one. "Dooggy." Then she points to her socks, "Diggy."

"*Slipper,*" my mother says, trying to get through to her one-and-a-half-year-old granddaughter.

"It's her sock. You're going to confuse her," I say. Olive points to her sock and proudly announces, "Duddy."

"She gets a lot of mileage out of those two words," my mother says, giving up.

"It's *five* words, actually," I explain.

Olive comes over and offers up her ripe little cheek for a kiss. If I bit it sweet juice would trickle down her face. Love opens in me, like time-lapse footage of flowers exploding into bloom. It knocks me over every time. I notice my mother across the room taking in her handiwork, her lineage, our six blue eyes all in a row, the life and limbs that sprung from her, and it occurs to me my mother loves me with the same force. A breath goes through me.

I pick my mother up for dinner. She opens the door and announces, "Well, that's it. I'm not buying any more things. It's enough now."

"Hi, Mom," I say.

"I'm finished," she kisses me on both cheeks, Beverly Roth–style. "I don't want any more things. I have enough things. It's my new thing. No more things. I want space. I want room." Then, very gravely, she adds, "We have too many things." Internally I agree with her. I'm sure Osama bin Laden does too. It is gross the consumer culture we live in. *Sex and the City* and Jimmy Choo and my obsession with Marc Jacobs everything and Costume International boots. Sure Sarah Jessica Parker canceled the series, but everyone knows she kept the shoes. She's no idiot. As usual my mother is ahead of the times. "Let's go," she says and grabs her coat—which happens to be a Jil Sander she didn't have last week.

"Nice coat," I say. "Is it new?"

Over dinner she tells me, like she always does, and always like the thought just occurred to her, "Life is about loss. It's just one loss after another. I've lost my brother, my husbands, my father, my mother . . ." she twirls her infamous red hair in her fingers. "It's just one loss after another. So you might as well get used to it. I think we should all be very Zen about it." On the way home she tells me, "By the way, I'm finished with Christmas. I'm not doing it anymore. I go to the spa anyway. Nobody wants to come home and I'm finished with the whole thing. Everyone can have something really smashing for their birthdays. Birthdays are fine but I'm through with Christmas. I hate Christmas and I'm not going to do it anymore. My mother always hated that we did Christmas. I think she died on Christmas eve deliberately. I think she did it on purpose. She hated that we did Christmas."

My daughter, who was supposed to spend her childhood basking in the warm glow of my idyllic maternal love, is having a time-out in the next room. And I am in a foul fucking mood about shit that has nothing to do with her.

Number one, I can't get an acting job. It's been over two years. The fancy agency that used to messenger me my scripts along with birthday and Christmas gifts from Tiffany, dropped me. I am now schlepping myself on the subway, uptown, to the Drama Bookshop (where I haven't been since I was an unemployed schlepper in acting classes looking for monologues) to pay for copies of the plays I have auditions for. Having an audition is now not only a pain in the ass and time-consuming, it is expensive. I am going broke, plus I am pretty sure I am not getting any little blue boxes this year during the holiday season.

Number two, I look my age for the first time in my life and I can't handle it. It is horrific. The ways my cheeks and eyes and jowls, not to mention my ass, don't stay up by themselves anymore are too numerous to think about without having a full-scale panic attack. I fantasize about having my eyes done while I heat up milk in the microwave. I catch myself gently tugging at my face, pulling at my cheeks, as I walk by anything shiny. I really think I would look so much better with some work and I hate myself for even considering it.

The war on my youth has begun. It's just a matter of time. My well-designed body was only meant to last one lifetime—just like everyone else's. At this moment it is just a vanity issue. I should be grateful because in the years to come it will become a deeper internal issue. So far my engine still works, it's just the paint that looks shabby. But one day when the engine stalls, my chassis cracks, wires short out for no apparent reason, the mechanic will just shake his head. "What do you want me to do?" he will say. "Things get old; they stop working."

And number three, there seems to have been a cosmic misunderstanding between me and the universe. My goal was to leave L.A., quit doing TV, and do quality theater in New York. But what happened is: I left L.A. and I no longer work. That was not the plan. I left because even though L.A. is a lush paradise, it was built in the middle of a desert and nothing growing there, be it flora or cup size, could exist left to its own natural devices. Everything and everybody is sustained by huge amounts of water and plastic surgery. I didn't want my child growing up surrounded by genuine phonies—crew members, producers, and network executives who tell you how *sweet* and *funny* and *pretty* and *crazy talented* you are as long as your name is on the call sheet in the morning. The truth about show people is that they have been phony for so long they honestly don't know how to be real. I wanted to come back to N.Y. I wanted to walk places. I wanted to see my daughter's face and hold her hand instead of looking at the back of her head in my rearview mirror because she was in her infant car seat facing backward. And I didn't want my child to witness me becoming a glorified punch line machine instead of the character actress that I am. I wanted Olive's mother to be real.

But I miss the money. I miss the shoes. *I really miss the money.* I am poor. I no like it, as Olive is fond of saying about almost everything these days.

ME, MYSELF, AND
I AM MY MOTHER

Olive and I are in the park with my mother. They are playing peekaboo. Olive is on the wobbly bridge and my mother is underneath looking up through the slats. My mother looks so happy; like a real grandmother. Olive is laughing. It's a genuine Kodak moment. I look around to see if any of my friends, the other mothers, are here. I want someone else to see how great my life is right now. Olive screams. I turn back around. She has fallen. I pick her up. In my arms I watch her eyes roll back in their sockets, her head go slack, her arms and legs twitch almost rhythmically. *This can't be real. This can't be happening,* I say to myself.

"Olive? Olive what is it? Are you okay? Oh my God, baby, are you all right?" Her eyes are on me, but she is looking through me. She is completely vacant. My daughter is in my arms in another dimension and I can't penetrate it. I take her to a bench and try to nurse her.

"What's she doing? Is she eating?" my mother says. I nod.

"What's she doing? Is she drinking?"

"YES," I say like I am speaking to a deaf person.

"She's all right. She's fine," she tells me.

"Yeah, I guess so, but that was so weird. She looked like she was having a seizure. It was so scary."

"She's fine, she doesn't even remember. There," she pokes her. "She's fine," she tells me again. "She's fine."

"Well I think I'm going to call the doctor."

"Nooohh, she's fine, she doesn't even remember. Do you? Peek-aboo. See, she's fine. She's forgotten all about it." For some reason this makes me feel neurotic and too emotional. "I'm not afraid she's traumatized," I say. "I just want to talk to a doctor. She's going to bed soon. I want to make sure she doesn't have a concussion."

"She's fine," my mother repeats, like I am crazy.

Two hours later the phone rings.

"What'd he say? How is she?" It is my mother. "What did the doctor say?"

"He said it sounded like she went into a little bit of shock and was probably fine and if we wanted to be really safe we should go to the emergency room, but he didn't think that was necessary so he said we should wake her up in a couple of hours and make sure she is 'rousable.' Which is excellent since she only started sleeping through the night two weeks ago."

Eight on the dot the next morning my mother calls.

"How is she?"

"She's fine."

"Good. I was so scared."

"You were?" I say. "Then why did you keep saying she's fine?"

"Because you were so frightened. I wanted to calm you down."

"I had no idea you were worried."

"Of course I was. I was absolutely terrified. But I didn't want us both to be."

I went to this day-care place everyone raves about. The one with the organic food and the yoga and the music classes. Everyone who is anyone in this neighborhood sends their kids there. Everyone but me. It looks like an old-age home to me. But instead of wheelchairs filled with lonely souls, waiting for their medication to kick in and their families to visit, there are a bunch of strollers filled with sad babies waiting for their moms to pick them up. I don't care how much organic food you serve, no one can convince me that a child would not rather be with his or her mother.

I will have my life back all too soon when she goes to school; I don't want to send her anywhere yet. But I could use a little bit of time to write. The woman running the place won't let me send Olive a few hours a few times a week. It is unhealthy, she said, for the children to be there less than fifteen hours a week. Bullshit. It is unhealthy for her wallet.

I finally got a job. I haven't worked since Olive was born. True, it is a third-rate Neil Simon play in Coconut Grove, Florida, but it's still show business. Costumes and makeup and glamour are still in my future. I have successfully put in thirteen months of solid mothering, and now I'm back. I've still got the chops. I am awesome.

It is hell. She screams when I leave and it rips right through me. I feel like Meryl Streep in *Sophie's Choice* as she is pried off of me. My husband yells at me, in front of her, that I am torturing her by telling her that I am leaving.

"Just go," he pleads. "She'll be fine. Don't make a big dramatic deal of it for Christ's sake."

"I'm not going to be one of those mothers that says, 'Come on honey, we're going to the circus' and instead we're going to the dentist to get a tooth pulled. I will not lie to her. 'Olive,' I explain every morning as I leave for rehearsal, 'I'm going to work now, but I'll be back later to say good night. Daddy's going to look after you. I love you, baby, and I'll see you later." She looks at me like I'm stabbing her in the heart. My husband starts yelling and I start crying. It's fucking agony.

Every other day I miss my exit on the freeway I am so upset.

We are all going crazy. She won't take a bath, she won't nap, she barely eats. She barely nurses. When she does nurse, I swear she does it as a courtesy, not because she wants to or needs my milk anymore. She thinks she's moved beyond me. She cries all the time. She has to be held constantly. She is a nightmare. She misses me and she is asserting herself. She doesn't know how to walk but she knows how to stage a protest. My husband is at the end of his rope. I can't wait to leave in the morning. I dread my day off. I would rather be on stage making people laugh and being clapped at than looking after my own child. I am a monster. I am my mother. I am not a mother. Then after a few weeks she adapts. She waves good-bye. She sleeps through the night again. She and Adam have the time of their lives. I kill myself to come home between matinees to see her and to be a good mother and I am about as interesting to her as a pile of spinach.

"There is no such thing as a free lunch," my mother always said. When I was twenty I had a pyramid meeting in her apartment. I gave them my $250 in exchange for the $10,000 they promised and she almost spit in my face. "There is no such thing as a free lunch," she told me then. It's true. You have to pay the piper. And if you don't spend time with the kid, they run to the person who does.

I am on the phone with my friend Corinne. "Wait," she says. "Yesterday, Barry was working at home and he promised me at two o'clock, when Stella went down for her nap, I could go out for a couple of hours. Alone."

"Excellent," I say. "What a guy that Barry turned out to be."

"Wait," she says. "So I put Stella down and I start putting on my coat and Barry says, 'I'm hungry. Could you make me a sandwich?'"

"You're kidding."

"Wait," she says. "And I say, 'Barry come on. You can make yourself a sandwich. There's turkey in there and bread.' 'Please?' he says. 'It tastes better when you make it. Pleeeaase?'"

"Oh my God. Is this my life?"

"I know. Wait," she says. "That's why I'm telling you this, so I tell him how annoying he is and how I've been waiting all week for my time—"

"Did you make him a sandwich?"

"Yeah, I made him a sandwich."

"Uh-huh. I would have too."

"I know. So I make him the sandwich and I remind him that I have been waiting all week for my time and how he promised me that today I could have some time, for myself, and he says, 'You want to read the story I wrote this morning?'"

"Oh my God. This is so my life."

"I know. Wait. So I say, 'No, Barry. This is my time. I'll read it later.' 'It'll take you ten minutes,' he says and I give him a really dirty look. Finally he says, 'Oh all right. You're right. Go on. Go. Have a nice time,' so I leave and forty-five minutes later—"

"No."

"Yes. Forty-five minutes later my cell phone rings and it's Barry and he says, 'Hi. What are you doing? You coming home soon?'"

"I can't believe it."

"I can't believe it either. Oh my God, did I tell you? I'm so tired I can't remember, I'm pregnant."

"You're kidding."

"No. I wish I was but I'm not."

"Jesus."

"I know."

"I didn't even know you had your period yet."

"You know it took me and Barry almost three years the first time. I figured it was gonna take a while this time too, so we thought we should start trying. But the first time out of the gate and there you have it."

"Wow."

"I know," she says. "Way to go, Barry."

"Way to go, Barry."

My mother rips a check out of her checkbook and slides it across the restaurant table. "Buddy," Olive says, looking up at me with a huge grin and eyes like blue lanterns. "Mo buddy," she says.

"What's she saying?"

"Butter. She wants more butter." I pass Olive another pat of butter. She laughs because happy things make her laugh. I laugh at jokes, not for joy. I am jealous. I look at the check my mother put in my hand. It's for five hundred dollars.

"Oh my God. Why?"

"Get yourself a babysitter. I know I said I'd babysit once a month. But November was crazy. Last week I forgot and this week is impossible and next week I have no time. The truth is I'm too tired. I can't do it." I knew she wouldn't do it.

Last month, she also forgot my husband's birthday and our anniversary. Two weeks later I got a message saying she was buying us a washer/dryer. I've been paid off most of my life. I put the check in my wallet. My mind is wading through the wonderful warm water of consumption. I am a consumer.

"What is this?" I ask my mother.

"It's nothing," she says grabbing the paper out of my hand. "Don't look at it," she tells me.

"Is it directions for tomorrow? Because if it is I should know." I am taking her to get a basal skin cancer removed from her nose in the morning.

"It's not for tomorrow. It's nothing."

"It's something. Is it from the procedure you had last week?"

"No. Cathy. For Christ's sake would you leave it alone?" She puts it on the table facing down, so I can't read it.

"It is directions on how to commit suicide, if you must know. It's from the Hemlock Society," she says.

"Why didn't you want me to know?"

"Because it's private."

"But it's not like I don't know you've been in touch with them. Why is it a secret?"

"Cathy, I don't have to discuss everything with you."

"Well I wish you would discuss this. It's not like I don't respect the decision. I told you twenty years ago I did. Why would you not want me to see it? I don't understand."

"Well I don't have to discuss it with you. I lost it. And then when I got the diagnosis of the skin cancer I found it."

"That must have been scary."

"I was scared, I guess."

"Let's put it somewhere safe." It comes out as though she were my child. All I want is for her to know I love her. I want to hug her and feel her in my arms. I want her to promise me that I am capable of surviving her death with grace and integrity. And I want her to promise me that I will be there, by her side, lovingly seeing her into the next world, counting out pills, fluffing pillows, taking care of her.

"I'll see you in the morning," she says instead. "Oh, here's a thing about my procedure." A three-page pamphlet on the procedure of removing basal skin cancer hits me in the arm.

I stand in her kitchen reading the pamphlet. When I was in college I used to come here, where I grew up, and steal food. Every time I left I filled a shopping bag with jam, tuna fish packed in olive oil, crackers, a couple of bananas. When I mentioned this to my husband recently he told me that stealing from one's mother was odd. But here I am standing in the kitchen, no longer a kid in college, and I'm still tempted to take something home with me, some toilet paper, anything. Recompense for not getting what I came for. Intimacy.

The next morning, my mother is terrified. We leave her apartment an hour and a half before her appointment, even though she only lives twenty blocks away from the hospital. There is an elderly couple already in the waiting room. They are the same age as my mother but that's where the similarity ends. Their wardrobe is Eddie Bauer and sensible shoes. My mother, by contrast, is wearing a Jil Sander suit and Prada shoes. The couple is very loud. He keeps shouting.

"*Henrietta. Over here!*" he yells for the tenth time. My mother tries to ignore them. She turns the pages of her *New York Times*, but I can tell they're aggravating her too much. She can't read. They have no idea how disruptive they are and it drives her crazy. I think it's touching. Henrietta's husband, who doesn't seem like he can take care of himself, is here at the doctor's office ready to take care of Henrietta.

The nurse calls my mother's name. I go in with her. They are very nice as they explain the procedure. After a local anesthesia, they will peel away tissue and examine it to determine if any cancer cells remain. If there are still cancer cells present they will do the whole procedure again until there are no more cancer cells. Each process of peeling and reviewing should take twenty to forty minutes. And while my mother waits for the results, she is supposed to sit in the waiting room with an ice pack on her nose to help control the swelling. When it's all done, they tell her, she will need to make an appointment with a plastic surgeon because they are going to carve a fairly significant hole in her nose. They ask her if she's ready, she says yes, and they give her the shot. I am sent back to the waiting room.

More people have arrived. A young Louis Vuitton–clad woman talks in Russian on her cell phone under a sign that says PLEASE REFRAIN FROM USING YOUR CELL PHONE. They call Henrietta's name. She goes in by herself because her husband has fallen asleep. I want to go in with her. I also want to tell the Russian to get off her goddamn phone. My mother emerges from the tissue-peeling room.

"Did you see my doctor?" she says, grinning. "She was so cute. Like you. She must be your age. She was adorable. Tiny. Like you. Mindy Meisel is her name. I liked her immediately. Let's get out of here."

"No, Mom. We have to wait. You have to sit here with your ice pack and we have to wait. Weren't you listening?"

"No. When?"

"When they explained the procedure. You don't remember?"

"No. What did they say?"

"We have to wait here until the films come back and they can see if they removed enough tissue and if they didn't then you have to have it done again."

"Again?"

"Yes, Mother. Jesus, they explained the whole thing to you."

"Well I wasn't listening. I didn't find it interesting. Should I get a plastic surgeon?"

"Oh, that part you remember?" I say. Henrietta emerges from a room with an ice pack on her nose, bumping into everyone and everything. Henrietta's husband wakes up in a panic. He doesn't know where she is. He starts yelling her name. People help them find each other. Poor Henrietta and her husband. They must be legally blind.

They call my mother's name again. We go in together. There are no more cancer cells. My mother is ecstatic. She hits the doctor in the leg and says, "I *told* you you were terrific. *I* could tell and *I* was right."

"So," the nurse says. "You have quite a deep wound and you need to go to a plastic surgeon."

"I don't want to go to a plastic surgeon."

"Are you sure?" the nurse says. "It's quite deep. Let me show you." She hands my mother a mirror.

"I don't want to see it and I don't want to go to a plastic surgeon. I changed my mind. I want Mindy to sew it up. She's spunky and I like her. I want her."

"Well, Dr. Meisel can sew it up, but she's not a plastic surgeon and you will have a scar."

"That's fine. I think scars are interesting. I like interesting faces. I want a scar. Let's go. I want Mindy to start sewing."

They ask me to go back to the waiting room while they sew her up. Another nurse tells me my mother needs to keep the cold compress on for at least twenty minutes and reapply it every twenty minutes for the next few hours. They recommend Advil for the pain and that she avoid alcohol for the next twenty-four hours so the blood from the incision has a chance to clot.

We leave Henrietta and her husband behind. My mother hasn't had a husband or a man for so long I can't imagine her any other way. She's a maverick who doesn't need anyone. She hails a cab waiting in front of the hospital not noticing the woman with a bandage wrapped around her head like a turban, hobbling toward the same cab. I try to steer my mother out of the way.

"What are you doing? I want to get in that cab."

"I know, but I think that other woman already hailed it."

"*What* other woman?" I don't bother explaining. I am as rude as my mother when I'm not with her. But in her presence I overcompensate for her lack of awareness. I'm at my best when I have something to act against.

She treats us to lunch at Artisanal. I order a glass of Côtes du Rhône. So does she.

"You're not supposed to have any wine."

"Why?"

"Because it interferes with your blood clotting. The nurse told me you shouldn't have any until tomorrow."

"Well that's ridiculous. I never drink wine."

"I know. But you never have enormous craters dug out of your nose either. Whatever. I'll have the grilled cheese and apple sandwich," I tell the waiter. "Please."

"So will I," she says. "I'll have the wine and go home and go to sleep. It will be fabulous." When the wine comes she tells me the story of her life again. How she read books incessantly and spent every day at the library discovering places other than Canada and plotting her escape. How she ended up marrying a man and making it as far as Toronto. I never knew my mother's first husband, but legend has it he was the love of her life. They had sex three times a day and as if that wasn't enough, he was kind and gentle to everyone he met. He died when she was twenty-eight. This is the legacy I grew up with.

My father was not the love of her life, and they didn't have sex three times a day. He was neurotic and brilliant and had a teenage daughter by the woman he was still married to when he met my mother. He was her boss. He was in love with her but she couldn't stand him. She had a series of illegal abortions, and the last one nearly killed her. My father came over every night to take care of her. He brought steak for her and presents for the kids. My mother believed he cared if she lived or died. It made an impression on her. He was desperate to marry her. She told him she didn't love him. He told her he loved her enough for both of them. She told him that was no way to go into a marriage. And then my father's psychiatrist told him he'd be crazy to marry her so my mother naturally said, "Let's do it." On their way to City Hall it was cold and raining and further legend has it my mother told my father if he didn't get a cab in five minutes the wedding was off. She meant it and he got a cab. They got married while my brother and sister threw water balloons out the window of the Stanhope Hotel. I was born two years later. She fell in love with him one year after that and eight years after that he too died.

We have another glass of wine.

"Mom, why didn't you want me to see those instructions last night?"

"Because, Cathy, that is the thing you don't understand about me. I am a very private person."

"But I've always told you everything."

"Yes, you have."

I have always told her everything. I called her every month from boarding school, terrified I was pregnant. I told her about every audition that was coming up knowing full well I would jinx it, and I then reported every job I didn't get. I told her how much less I was being paid in comparison to all the other actors on whatever series I was doing. I told her every detail about why my first marriage didn't last. I never understood people who edited what they told their parents. I thought my frankness made us close. I was always proud of that closeness. A lifetime of spilling my guts passes before my eyes, and I see what I never saw before. It's so obvious. I have been telling her everything and she doesn't want to know. She's listened, but it's made her uncomfortable. I am so embarrassed.

"You want me to be something I'm not," she continues. "You are a romantic. I'm not. It's not possible for me. I admire you. You want to be close to everyone but I know things now that make it impossible."

I take her home in a taxi and put her to bed. She tells me to go home and take care of my daughter. She'll be fine. She just wants to go to sleep. I wait in the kitchen a few minutes to make sure she's okay. I hear her dial the phone.

"Beverly? I'm fine. Yes. They got it out. I know! I'm so relieved. My doctor was fabulous." She calls four other friends in rapid succession and finally goes to sleep. I get on the phone and call my brother and my sisters. They have been on pins and needles all day. Leslie is furious.

"Why didn't *she* call?"

"I don't know, I guess she's tired."

"I've been waiting by the phone all morning. I can't believe her."

I hang up and it hits me. I have misinterpreted the story of her life. I got it wrong my entire life. I always thought the "people" she couldn't be close to were the rest of the world. But "people" was code for us, the people who loved her most: her children.

My husband and I didn't get invited to a dinner party. We feel snubbed.

"Maybe it's a small party," I say.

"Fuck it," he says. "I don't want to invite anybody over anymore. I mean nobody ever invites us anywhere."

"Maybe it was like when we didn't invite Doug and Sandy because we just assumed they couldn't get a babysitter and we didn't have enough chairs anyway."

"I don't know. When I asked Ted what he was doing tonight he was just all weird and obviously uncomfortable."

"So maybe you should ask him about it. Maybe he can tell us why we are so undesirable." He glares at me, reminding me that *I* am the difficult one.

"It's not me this time," I say. "I swear. I get along fine with her. We are totally patched up. Really."

"Well I guess it's me then." But I can tell he doesn't think so. He tells me he'll mention it to Ted again and see what he can dig up. We may be broke and hardly have sex because we share a room with our two-year-old, but at least he will get back on track socially.

"Did you ever talk to him?" I ask a few days later.

"Mmhmm. He like deliberately did not try to make me feel better."

"Did you tell him your feelings were hurt? Because sometimes you're not that direct."

"Yes, I said, 'It really hurt my feelings that we didn't get invited to Penelope's dinner party. We've had her over like five times.'"

"What'd he say?"

"He just said, 'Oh' or something."

"Maybe you should tell him it makes you feel weird that he never tries to make you feel better."

"No, I think I'll just do nothing."

"But maybe it would help."

"No, Cathy. It only makes it worse. People do not like to be picked apart. They like to be left alone."

"But if you have a chance to get closer, wouldn't you want to?" I ask him.

"No. Because it never makes you closer. It makes people pull away."

"Sometimes it doesn't."

"Very rarely, Cathy," he says. I feel like a child with a withered leg whose parents console by saying it is beautiful.

"You tell me things that are hard to hear and I try and change and we get closer," I say.

"Yes we do, but that is totally different. We are intimate."

"I thought you were intimate with Ted."

"I just want to get along with him as well as possible."

"But why don't you want to get along better?"

"Because I have lower expectations than you do, Cathy. I just want my relationships to be easy."

"I just want to get closer and make things go deeper."

"That is not what most people want. They just want to get along."

"I always thought that was the same thing."

"No, Cathy," he says.

"She really is the best mother I know. You know a lot of her friends had ideas about how they wanted to be and I swear she is the only one of them who is really doing it." This is my fucking husband talking. I have just put a perfectly grilled red snapper on the table, and he is saying these nice things about me, to company. I am a good mother and Olive is having the childhood I dreamed of. I listen to her. I don't abuse my power. She is never pawned off on other people. I care about her and she knows it. But who knows what she will remember.

I never knew my mother's mother. Only about her. I knew she ran away from Russia by herself at nine years old. She fended for herself, learned English, and escaped being married, at twelve, to a bald man she didn't like. She was a survivor. My grandfather had seven brothers and they were fur trappers and cowboys. I didn't get to know him either.

I worry Olive is too young to remember my mother. I worry she will only know about her. That her Bubbe was an amazing woman who never went to college but ran a department at a major university. A woman who was married and widowed twice. A woman who grew up with one pair of shoes and grew into Jil Sander suits and a house in Bridgehampton and business class to Europe four times a year. A woman who lived to work and went to the White House, because of her work, under three separate administrations. I didn't know my Bubbe either. Just the legend.

It is eleven hundred degrees. We're going to the sandbox. It's always cool in the sandbox even if it's germy. I hang Olive's bucket and shovel on the stroller and we're out the door.

"Bucka," she says.

"That's right, it's your bucket." I smile at her and she nods her head up and down like a maniac.

"Bucka," she says, still delighted.

"That's right."

"Bucka."

"I know it's your bucket," I laugh.

"Bucka," she tells me again.

"Yup. It's your bucket."

"Bucka." The word "chatterbox" leaps to mind. My daughter is like a set of those fake teeth that clatter up and down. It's incredible how many times she can say the same word. I always answer her. I think it's rude not to. She's talking to me. I don't understand how people can ignore babies. I really don't. They just ignore them like they're not there, as though they're not people. And yet I have no idea how I can keep up this particular conversation either. The sandbox is still eight blocks away.

"Hey, look," I say pointing up ahead. "There's a dog." That always gets her. She loves a dog.

"Puh*pea*," she says correcting me.

"Yeah," I say. "It's a black puppy."

"Moomay," she says.

"Yup, it's a woman with a puppy. A woman in a nice flowered dress, I might add."

"Wowuh."

"Flowers," I agree. "Oh my." We carry on like this until we reach our destination. Olive has never been in the sandbox barefoot before. She puts her toes in very slowly. She gives it a lot of thought. I love watching her. Out of nowhere a frenetic boy, a candidate for Ritalin if I ever saw one, arrives. "*Hey hey hey is this yours?*" he asks. I manage to dodge his brightly colored wheelbarrow before it mows me down.

"No."

128

"No?" he says. *"Is it hers?"*

"No. It was here when we got here." He cannot believe a kick-ass toy like this could just be here for the taking. He starts flying back and forth like a bug caught in a jar. *"Is this yours?"* He shouts at random. No one pays any attention. He begins an intense mission: taking sand out of the sandbox and putting it in the wheelbarrow and dumping it on the ground outside the sandbox. After the third load I say, "You can't do that. You have to leave the sand in the sandbox." He ignores me. I don't like him. He's a little bully.

I tell him again. "Hey, you need to leave the sand in the sandbox so other people can play with it. If you want to load stuff in your wheelbarrow go over there to that pile of dirt." He still ignores me. I have no idea what I'm going to do if he doesn't listen to me. If I wasn't bigger than him I wouldn't dare tell him anything. Because I'd be scared of him. I'm scared of him now. He's scary. And he has a long string of snot hanging from his left nostril. That he doesn't have a Kleenex or use his sleeve or even his hand to get rid of it is simply mesmerizing to me. The snot is just dangling there. Every time it reaches his lip he breathes it back in. It slithers in and out of his nose four times, before I will myself not to look anymore. "Seriously," I tell him, eyes looking at the ground. "You have to stop doing that. It's not fair for the kids playing in the sandbox. There's not gonna be any sand left for them." He throws his shovel down really hard and starts running around the edge of the sandbox aggressively throwing sticks and miscellaneous toys in. I really don't like this kid one bit. He's mean.

"You use a belt ta hit huh?"

"What?"

"You use a belt ta hit huh with?"

"What are you talking about?"

"No?" he says in total disbelief.

"No."

"What you hit huh with?"

"I don't hit her." He looks at me like I'm out of my mind.

"*You never hit huh?*"

"No," I tell him.

"But when she's bad?"

"No. I never hit her." He runs away to wreak havoc somewhere else.

There's big trouble in our local park. A mother saw a nanny throw a wet wipe into the bushes and suggested that she use a garbage can instead. The nanny suggested that the mother go fuck herself, and it just sort of escalated from there.

"It's terrible," I say as I push Olive in the swing. "Wheee."

"It's awful," Regina says as she pushes Owen. "It's awful and to say that in front of the kids . . . Wheee. But Trish definitely said things she shouldn't have either, like she told the nanny, after the nanny told her that her husband was fucking his secretary, she said, 'Oh, yeah, well you don't even know your own kids you're so busy looking after someone else's.'"

"Jesus," I say, absentmindedly stroking Olive's bald head. She's twenty-one months old and the back of her head still looks like it did the day she was born. They handed me a mirror so I could watch what I was trying to push out of me and all I saw was this swirl of dark hair. It is such a familiar and gorgeous sight. I love it. "Jesus," I say again.

"I know," Regina says. "It's really depressing there's that much tension. I try and pretend there isn't. But obviously there is."

"Well I never knew there was," I say. "I swear." Regina looks at me like I'm nuts. "I never even thought about any tension," I continue. "I spend more time with the nannies than I do with the mothers."

"I know what you mean," Regina says. I look at Regina like

she's nuts. Regina has a nanny. What does she know? This is the first time I've seen Regina in the park in weeks.

The next day it's hot as hell. There are four nannies and a bunch of strollers parked in front of a bench in the shade.

"Let's go over there in the shade," I tell Olive. She waddles along next to me but I surprise myself and keep walking past the nannies. I feel like they're looking at me as if they don't like me. I don't feel welcome with the nannies. I feel paranoid. It's kind of how I felt all through high school.

Olive and I get our paraphernalia organized and I try to act normal. But it's hard to do normal when there's a black cloud of tension hanging over your head. Olive wants me to trace her body with chalk. She lies down on the ground and sticks her arms and legs out while I outline her. She loves it but I think she's afraid it might hurt since she always closes her eyes until I say, "All done." Suddenly we have a crowd. We're popular. I swear I wish I knew then what I know now. Chalk. If I had known to carry chalk when I was little I would never have been lonely.

All the kids want a turn. They're all lying down, getting traced, and the older ones use different colors to draw their clothes on. It's excellent and Olive loves the bigger kids. They thrill her. She sees a bigger girl drawing her dress on her chalk body, so Olive takes a piece of chalk and draws a couple of straight lines where her foot is and claps. I trace a girl named Daisy and her sister Georgia and then their friend Megan lies down and I'm about to do her when her nanny's voice bellows, *"Megan get up off the floor now!!!!!"* Megan gets upset. So do I. I don't want to get in trouble with the nanny. Megan jumps up. She looks at me. I apologize and she lies down again. I tell her, "Listen, I don't know if that's a good idea. You should probably get permission. Okay?" She looks over at her nanny and then she looks at me and she says, "You ask her."

"Well I'll go with you but I think you should ask her."

"Okay, come with me," she says.

"Okay. I'll come with you."

"And you ask her," she tells me.

"No *you ask* her. I'll go with you. But you ask her." Megan's nanny scares me. I'm not asking her. We're on our way over when her nanny appears out of nowhere and picks Megan up by the seat of her size 3T skort and says, "*Don't you be lying down on the ground and getting dirty. What's the matter with you?*" She's got a loud and lyrical roar. She starts smacking the leaves off her charge's behind in a demonstration of how dirty it is. I'm so glad I don't have a nanny anymore.

I am five. "I can't feel you," I whine at my mother. "I can't feel you." She holds my hand so floppy. I squeeze hers. "Cathy, stop it, I can't stand it when you hang on me. Stop hanging." She says *hanging* like there are four *G*'s in the word. "Squeeze," I plead. When Olive gets older she holds my hand really loose and says, "Is that how your mother did it?" She thinks it's really funny.

Olive and I are on a field trip to the children's zoo in Central Park. I came here every day as a kid. It's possible I'm more excited about being here than she is.

"Olive, look at the bunnies."

"Oh my," she says.

"That one with the floppy ears is my favorite. Look at him. I love them with the floppy ears!"

"Kwoot," she says.

"I know it's so cute."

We walk over to the goats. I show her how to put the quarters in the gumball machine filled with goat pellets. She wants to eat some.

"No, honey," I say smoothing her dark brown hair, "that's for the goats. That's their food. Olive, look at those goats, that's where your milk comes from sometimes. What do you think of that?"

"Goat."

"Yup, goats all right. See their funny beards?"

"Beer."

We walk on the lily pad path across the duck pond and stand in front of a fence that has holes cut out at various eye levels for small children. She peeks through at the ducks.

"Quack," she says jumping up and down. "Quack."

"Quack quack," I say.

New York is magic. I don't know how anyone could raise a child anywhere else. I don't care what anyone says. I love it. Olive is standing next to a little boy who has almost mastered standing. He is with his grandmother, who must be close to eighty. She is crouching on the ground next to him and whatever damage she is doing to her joints is completely offset by how happy she is to be with him. The little boy is very wobbly. Olive and I watch him totter, until he finally tips over. He looks up at his grandmother, bewildered, and starts crying. She strains, somehow managing to lift him up. She starts dusting the leaves off him when his mother appears like a bat out of hell and snatches her son out of her mother's arms.

"What are you doing?" she yells. I feel sorry for her mother. She looks hurt and confused. It must be disconcerting to be yelled at by your own child. "He needs to be *held*, not *cleaned*," the daughter continues. "Here I am, sweetheart. Here I am. Here I am. Mommy's here. Oh, my sweetheart, I'm so sorry I wasn't here for you. Mommy's here." The air between them is filled with the debris of a lifetime's worth of disappointments. That poor woman is nuts. I am fucking nuts. Families are all fucking nuts. Children don't stand a chance.

"Pant, oh my." Olive says, walking around the backyard looking at the flowers.

"Bewd, oh my. Tee. Oh my."

"That's right, plants and birds and trees. Oooh Olive, there's a squirrel."

"Oh my," she says.

Olive loves life. Every morning I come to get her and she is standing in her crib, smiling, arms out, ready. "Wake up, do things," she tells me as I pick her up and kiss her everywhere. It is a beautiful way to be. My attitude, on the other hand, has stunk for as long as I can remember. I want to be fascinated by a string bean and delighted with a paper towel. I also want to know what I am supposed to do about not having a viable escape plan and a survival kit in place for the next terrorist attack; global warming; the fact that many species of frogs are becoming extinct and some species of female fish are mutating into male fish, not to mention a million other environmental horror stories; being a citizen of a country where people can't bear to make a sacrifice, driving Hummers as though oil is not a commodity they need to worry about, turning up the air-conditioning every summer, not understanding that something's got to give or there will be yet another blackout, going on about their consumer business as though people's children are not dying in a war we have no business fighting; being American, which in my lifetime has gone from something to be envied all over the world to something downright shameful. Not to mention preschool, which I am not signed up for, and couldn't afford even if I was. Of course I am up nights. Of course I have a bad attitude.

Today we got up. We cuddled before we got dressed. We had breakfast. We went out in the yard and investigated some bark, smelled some hyacinths, drew a picture with a rock on the concrete, examined some worms. I made a couple of phone calls. She played with her cars and washed the walls. We had more breakfast. We made a vat of macaroni and cheese to freeze. She sprinkled the cheese. We read A. A. Milne. She did some work with refrigerator magnets. We hung out. It was one of the nicest mornings of my life.

Should I have taught her how to count to a hundred?

Olive is pretending to drive. She's turning one of the two steering wheels attached to the jungle gym at the park.

"I are driving," she tells me.

"Excellent," I say.

"I are driving acouse it's too far a walk."

"Where are we going?" I ask.

"To the museum of natural histreet."

"Goody," I say. "Will you tell me when we get there? Because I don't want to miss it. I love the museum of natural history."

"I will, Mama," she assures me. And I believe her. There is another little boy playing nearby. I've seen him around. He has a full head of hair but he barely speaks. He goes to the organic day care three days a week. Olive looks like a baby next to him because she still has so little hair. His mother smiles at me. I've seen her before too. I'm not attracted to her. And her kid seems boring. I want to move to a groovier neighborhood. Sometimes Olive and I go to Washington Square Park to visit my mother and I am in awe of all the good-looking mothers there who wear a little makeup and have nice haircuts and styly outfits. There's no one like that here. I touch my hair that hasn't been cut in almost a year and that I barely ever wash. I suddenly feel like a housewife.

———

Today I had two auditions. I went out for lunch with a friend and to the Met instead of coming home in between. I felt like a regular person enjoying the city, no sippy cup in my purse, a little makeup on my face. I had fun, so naturally I panicked. *I am evil. I like being away from her.* I tormented myself. *I want a full-time nanny. I have lost all my maternal instincts. I don't want a child.* It is such a fine line between self-preservation and neglect of others, between good intentions and utter insanity.

I got a part in a movie. It's only a twenty-minute short and I'm not being paid, but it's an action movie. I run through the woods, I get shot, and then I die. I set the alarm every day before Olive wakes up and I don't get home until she's in bed, or I fall asleep in bed while my husband is reading to her. I am exhausted. How do people work? Why do people work? Because they need the money. Because they like it. But how can you like two completely different things (your work and your children) that threaten to destroy each other? I would die if I didn't have a husband to fill in for me. If I had a nanny I would probably fantasize during the day about never coming home and dream at night about killing her because I thought Olive was too attached to her.

I was so happy to take this job instead of my old sitcom job that required me to enter frame, announce the joke, and then exit. Sure it is a nonpaying job, but who cares, it could turn out really great and I have always wanted to work in this genre. I am watching the video playback. It will show my big emotional journey. My husband getting shot and dying in my arms and then the running part happens. I run from the hunters who inadvertently shot my husband because I think they are after me too. I can't wait. I feel like Diana Rigg in *The Avengers*. I felt so tough when we were shooting. It was amazing. Oh God. I run like such a girl. I run like a fairy with a sore toe prancing through the woods. I don't look anything like an action star. Or any kind of star.

I didn't die effectively. My eyes kept fluttering. It was the last shot of the day, we were losing light, and we had to wrap. I let the twenty-minute, nonpaying, action-movie-making team down.

I'm starting to wonder if I'm really cut out for show business. The preoccupation with self that runs rampant in the business of show is awful. Even though I am pretty preoccupied myself. I never felt noticed and now I'm making up for it. It's pretty basic. I am a slob (I leave evidence of myself everywhere), I am rude (like my mother), I cut people off verbally and physically, I am mostly unaware of others and my impact on them. Except for Olive. Where Olive is concerned I am like a contestant on a game show, the itchy one who buzzes before the question is even asked. I am so tuned in to her it is embarrassing. I see other parents act like this and I feel sorry for them. *Get a life*, I think and I sound like my mother who always said you can't live through your children. "That's what my sister did. Now look at her."

My aunt Phyllis entered my cousin Vicky in a beauty contest when Vicky was sixteen. Winning that contest was my aunt's entire reason for living. She made Vicky practice at home in her bathing suit and pumps. She got Vicky singing and elocution lessons. She bought Vicky an entire new wardrobe. She was determined to win that contest. The day before the event, she had Vicky's hair done professionally. When they got home she realized she couldn't get Vicky undressed without ruining her hair, so she cut Vicky's dress off her with scissors. My mother says, "With *scissors* she cut that dress off her. I will never forget it."

The moral is: you cannot live through your children because they grow up and you're left with nothing. My aunt never had other interests. Vicky was it. My mother always had other interests. Even before she started working again after my father died it was obvious that taking care of us was not at the top of her list of interests. Writing is becoming an interest of mine. But it is not a career, yet. I used to have a career with acting. But shortly after I left the theater company and my speechwriter playwright boyfriend I lost the pleasure of it. I started getting highly paid, which was very distracting. First-class airfare works wonders on getting one's mind off deeper ambitions. Then I staved off depression with things money could buy: yoga and shopping and a rigorous skin-care routine. But the mendacity of the entertainment world took its toll. The pleasure was no longer in the process or in the work. It was in landing the job, not in doing the job. I was like some guy on the make who lives to score. And I kept scoring, but my heart wasn't in it. The scripts and the directors were bad, and even if they were good, my part was so small the lighting on the lead's nose was more important than my performance. Most of my good takes ended up on the floor. I learned to detach or else my precious little artist heart would get broken.

Last month I shot a commercial, which is all I have left of my acting career. I went to Columbus, Ohio. I stayed at a nice hotel and I smoked multiple cigarettes without fear of discovery by child or husband, which was a luxury. I fell asleep reading in bed, which is another luxury because my husband and I are roommates with our daughter and we never get to do anything in our room anymore but sleep. The next day I showered and read the paper, two other former luxuries. I shopped (in the store we were shooting in) while I waited for my scene to be ready, did my takes, and flew home. I didn't do a very good job. In fact I phoned it in. But I told myself, *it's just a commercial.*

Flying back I realized this is all I am capable of. If I can't talk to anyone on the phone when Olive is around how can I do a good job on a Value City commercial? If I can't talk to my own husband when she is in the room, how can I focus on preparing really well for an audition? Natasha Richardson stayed in a hotel while she was rehearsing *Streetcar Named Desire*. If she didn't think she could prepare while being around her family, who am I kidding? And Blanche DuBois is a much better role than Holiday Shopper in Discount Store—or joke vehicle in a sitcom.

Olive comes first. I don't want to be pulled. I cannot fight the pull. I have friends who work full-time; they always talk about the pull. The pull is that thing that you love in addition to your kids. The more I am with Olive the better and easier it is. It is a piece of cake until I pursue an outside interest and go away, even for an hour. Once I go away the littlest bit, the pull rolls in. It has a dangerous undertow. In its wake I forget how to swim. In its presence I am afraid of the water. I begin to drown. I go down like a sinking ship.

"What are you doin', Mom?" Olive says standing up in her crib.

"I'm going to get you some water."

"*Why*, Mom?"

"Because you asked me to."

"*Why*, Mom?"

"I guess because you're thirsty."

"*Why*, Mom? *Why?*"

"Olive, is this a shenanigan?"

"*No,*" she says indignantly. "I are coughing." She coughs a little. It's a total shenanigan.

"Oh my God. You are driving me crazy."

"*Why*, Mom? What are you doin', Mom?"

"I'm looking for your sippy cup so I can get you some water so you can take a nap and stop bossing me around, that's what I'm doing. Is your cup downstairs? Where's your cup?"

"Can I come? I want to come."

"No, honey."

"Why, Mom?"

"Because it's nap time."

"Is it a day nap or a night nap?"

"It's a day nap."

"I want come too. I want come too!"

"Olive, for Christ's sake. Come on. No more shenanigans."

"I want come too. This will be the last shanagin!"

"*No.* No more shenanigans."

"Why? Mom?"

"*Because* I can't handle it anymore, that's why. Get into bed. Please."

"But I'm not mad at you," she sings to me.

"I know, honey. I'm the one who's getting mad."

"Why, Mom?"

"Because you are being a pain in the ass, that's why."

I am driving. Olive is in the backseat, alternating between screaming or crying. It's two and a half more hours, at least. If we run into traffic or get a flat tire I don't know what I'll do. Suicide is always an option, but I haven't had the discipline thus far and now I am the mother of a person whom I would miss too much to try it. I know I should be sitting in the backseat entertaining her, but her father made me promise I would drive to the Hamptons instead of my mother. It's her car and her house but he doesn't like his mother-in-law's driving. He has a point. My mother's position on driving is this: nervous drivers are terrible drivers. "You will be a good driver," she began telling me when I was five. "You will drive with confidence. There is nothing more irritating than a nervous driver, Cathy. Carly is a nervous driver. I hate driving with Carly."

My mother is, of course, a confident driver. She backed off the on-ramp to the Long Island Expressway last weekend with total confidence. She nearly killed us, but she was very confident. "Mow 'em down" is basically her style of driving. And she has gotten more confident the bigger her SUVs get. She's mad at me because she's not driving and I'm mad at my husband because I have to make up a cockamamy story that I do not have time to go into about why I am driving and Olive's mad at everyone because she doesn't like being in the car and she is really constipated. It's going to be a good weekend.

"*Aaaaaahhhhh!* My poopy! *Help* me." She hasn't pooped in four days. This is the fourth time in a year I've given her laxatives. It is starting to make me very nervous.

"Olive," I say. "I know it hurts, honey. But I promise it will come out. Just try and let it. I promise it will come out. Remember how it came out the last time?"

"Aaaahahhhhh. My tushie. My tushie. My tushie. My tushie. *Ahhhahhhh*. I want sit on your lap."

"I know, lovey, but you can't because I'm strapped into my seat belt and you're strapped into your car seat. As soon as we get to Bubbe's you can sit on my lap. Okay?"

"*Aahhhhhhhhhhhh.*"

"I know, honey."

"Olive, look out the window," my mother instructs to the backseat.

"No, my tushie."

"Okay, that's enough. Don't think about it. Oh, look at the red truck. Do you see the red truck?"

"Help. My *tushie!*" she screams.

"Ohhh. It's so bad. You poor thing. Just try and let it out," I say glaring at my mother.

"That's enough, Cathy. You're making it worse," my mother tells me.

"How am I making it worse? She hasn't shit in four days. She's in agony."

"If you ignore it, it will pass. Just stop thinking about it. Stop thinking about it, Olive."

"You think I am indulging her?"

"Yes," she tells me. "Olive do you know what I see?"

"My poopy!"

"Olive, don't think about it," my mother tells her as though being constipated is simply a state of mind.

"Mom, she's not making it worse. What are you talking about?"

"We have a different philosophy," my mother says.

"Yes, we do. I believe in acknowledging it. And *then* letting it go. She is in pain. There's no use pretending that's not so. What is the point of pretending?"

"We have a different philosophy."

"Yes, we certainly do," I say.

We are in complete agreement.

Shopping for back-to-school clothes, my mother says, "Achh, they're too big," while she sticks her hand all the way down a pair of Danskins I am trying on. "They're swimming on you," she declares and opens the curtain, exposing me, with no shirt on and her hand shoved down my behind, for the rest of the shopping public to see. She shouts to the saleslady for the next smaller size. "She's swimming in them, you better bring the five! The six is swimming on her!"

"We don't have the ones with flowers in her size," the saleslady calls back. "Just the plain navy, and here's a top you might be interested in." My mother is still holding the curtain open. "I don't care for the top," my mother shouts. Finally she leaves to find the saleslady and talk to her in person without yelling across the 4–6X department in Bloomingdale's. The curtain closes behind her. I breathe deeply. My heart slows down until my mother whisks open the curtain again. She has returned with yet another navy shirt, and I am again exposed.

"Can you close the curtain?" I ask her.

"What for?" my mother says as if that is the most ridiculous request she ever heard.

"Because I'm in here."

"Don't be ridiculous."

"Mom."

"Nobody's looking at you. What do you care? What do they care? No one cares about your body. Don't be ridiculous, Cathy."

"You don't leave the curtain open when you try on clothes," I point out, huddled in the corner, trying to hide.

"Well I would. But I'm a woman with breasts and people are uncomfortable about that sort of thing. And they happen to be wrong. People's bodies are perfectly natural things. You have a fabulous bod. You've got nothing to be ashamed about."

"Please!" I beg.

"Oh for Christ's sake, Cathy!"

"Please," I say again on the verge of tears. My mother looks at me like I am crazy and closes the curtain. But it is not really a victory because in my mother's mind I just traded my right to privacy for an admission of complete insanity.

I haven't exercised in almost three years. And I am taking sleeping pills. These things worry me. Also preschool. Filling out the applications. Going on the tours. Doing the research. The cost of preschool. Whether or not I can even handle sending her to preschool when I can barely leave her in day care for six hours a week. I lie awake every night waiting for my sleeping pill to kick in pretending that I am not troubled by anything. I am trying to reconcile working with being a mother. I am a wreck. And I am so tired

I think I am going to collapse. I lose my patience. I can't bear to lose my patience with her when she hasn't done anything that warrants it. Everyone says, "Cathy, you're human." But I want to be the kind of human who wakes up tired in the morning and says, "Yay! I'm tired! I'm so lucky to have so many wonderful things in my life making me tired! A great job, a wonderful child! Who cares about the state of the world? I'll just put some makeup on and have an extra cup of coffee and be thankful." I have never been that kind of human.

I stayed up all night working on the application for Friends. I got teardrops all over it. I love that school. I have no idea how we will pay for it, but I don't care. I will worry about it after. We went to the cocktail parties, the mixers, we showed our smiling faces, we did everything eager prospective parents must do; and we smiled the whole time. Friends doesn't have computers until the second grade because they think they are antisocial; they have quiet time every day for reflection. The art on the walls in there is unbelievable. Older kids are assigned a younger kid to look out for all year. I love it. It is a perfect school and she can stay there until college. I am so relieved. I will not let Adam write the essay. If he wrote it and we didn't get in I would never forgive him.

Olive changed her name to Tweety. "I are Tweety," she said. That was all there was to it. The next day she told me that I was Sylvester. "You are Toolester," she said. It's been this way for three weeks now. Tonight when she wakes up (for some unknown reason), I beg her to go back to sleep, just like I did when she was Olive.

"Can I get up? Mom? Can I wake up?"

"No, Tweety," I look at the clock. It's four in the morning. "It's the middle of the night!"

"Why?"

"Because it's not morning yet. Not enough time went by. Look, it's still dark."

"When it's morning can I get up?"

"Yes, honey, of course you can. Now please go back to sleep because we need sleep or we'll be crabby."

"Mom?"

"Tweety, please go back to sleep. We'll talk in the morning. I promise."

"Mommy?"

"Oh my God, Tweety. Please."

"Mommy? Are you driving crazy?"

"Yes. You're driving me crazy. Please go to sleep. I'm going back to sleep. Good night, honey."

I put the covers on her and it occurs to me that I am having a serious conversation with a person named Tweety. When I drop her off at day care the next morning we press the buzzer and Olive tells the intercom, "It's Tweety." They buzz us in but at some point one of the Polish women forgets and says, "Good morning, Olive," and Olive has to correct her. "*No*, I changed my name a Tweety!" The other kids have a hard time calling her Tweety too. But Olive does not waver in her commitment to her new name and yells at them until they get it right. In the park we are playing with someone new and she asks Olive what her name is.

"Well," Olive says to the girl's mother, "I like a call myself Tweety."

Two more weeks pass. "Come on, Tweety. Dinner's ready," I say. It just rolls off my tongue like nothing. I miss the name Olive. In theory I miss it more because I prefer the name Olive to the name Tweety, but on a daily basis I am surprisingly used to it. I ask her if she will ever be Olive again. "Mmn-hnmm," she says, but she does not give any indication when. A friend points out what a WASPy-sounding name Olive's chosen for herself. She says it is a name like

Dabber or Muffit. I try to imagine Olive as a young woman, sitting in her office writing notes to people on memo pads that say "From the Desk of Tweety Forgash." This starts to make me nervous.

The next morning she tells me that she's changed her name again.

"Oh boy," I say, trying not to sound relieved. "What is it?"

"Spot," she says.

We didn't get in. I cannot believe it. My hands shook when I opened the letter. I am still shaking. I am indignant and there is nothing my mother the big shot can do unless she becomes a Quaker. Maybe I will become a Quaker. It's okay. I will apply again next year. I didn't even like their preschool as much as the older school. I am applying every year until we get in. We will get in next year.

My in-laws are coming for dinner. I am flat on my back, in bed, sick as a dog. But Adam is a dreamboat and goes with Olive to buy all the groceries while I sleep. When I wake up I see him at the stove cooking the sausages. I look at the bag they came in and do a double take. I can't believe what I see. He didn't buy them from the Sausage King. We live in the sausage capital of the world and he may as well have bought microwaveable breakfast links.

"Adam. Why didn't you buy them at the Sausage King?"

"Because I was in the cheese store buying the bread and they had them so I thought I'd try them."

"Are they the fennel ones?"

"No. They didn't have the fennel ones."

"Oh, Jesus."

"You know what, Cathy?" he says throwing the wooden spoon on the counter. "Do it yourself. You're a fucking pleasure to help."

I'm in a pickle. I know he's right. But on the other hand he did buy and pay for inferior sausage product. We're cooking a sausage ragout. Sausage is the main ingredient, and it's corrupted. I go in his office and try to apologize.

"I'm sorry. I should have just been thanking you. That was so nice of you to do the shopping. Really. I just don't understand how you could not go to the Sausage King. It's right next door to the cheese store. When they didn't even have the fennel ones why didn't you just think to go next door?"

He starts yelling at me. He accuses me of torturing him. He's pounding his finger into the desk to illustrate how I pretend to apologize and then continue to stick it to him. Part of me thinks, *Fuck it*. I'm fussy about food and if that is the price the world has to pay for me getting over an eating disorder then so be it. But, I've heard this before. I've seen the finger-pounding-into-the-desk gesture before. They tell me I am a bully. The speechwriter explained to me, in a museum after I kept showing him a painting I loved over and over, that he saw it the first time and he didn't like it. "You seem to think," he told me, "that if you continue to explain to me in different words why you like it that I will change my mind. I saw the painting, I heard why you like it, and I still don't like it. So quit making me go back and look at it. I'm looking at my own stuff."

It is true. I think everyone will see things my way if I just explain them properly. So I keep explaining. I keep talking. I keep trying. The speechwriter told me I was a bully. I left him because he was a bully. My husband thinks I am the biggest bully ever. But I never bully Olive. She is the only person in the world I have nothing but patience for. I never take my frustration out on her. I treat everyone else as though common courtesy was reserved for special occasions. I am rude and nasty without even realizing or without feeling like I have it in me to be otherwise. I wonder if I would make her feel bad about getting the wrong sausages. No, not her. It is the rest of the human race I can't seem to get along with.

Every night after dinner Olive and I go on a walk. We look for the moon and we marvel at all the crazy Christmas decorations over-populating the front yards of our Italian neighborhood. They used to drive me crazy but now I can't wait until they go up. The colored lights that twinkle and the illuminated reindeer that move and the carols coming from tinny hidden speakers turn our street into an electronic wonderland. It's cold and we are bundled up and Olive can barely walk in her snowsuit but we hold hands and look at everything.

"Oh moon?" Olive calls. "Oh moon? Where is de moon, mumma?"

"Maybe it's behind some clouds," I offer.

"Maybe it goed to see some stars," she says.

"Oh my God. I bet you're right. That is so good." She is so much smarter than me. So much sweeter and truer than me, than anyone I know. I hold on tight to her mitten. It is so squishy, her mitten, I wonder if her hand is even in there.

"I love you, Olive."

My mother—who never went to college and who is the chairman of a department at NYU she "made up out of her head" in the seventies—is on the phone. She is sitting in her corner office under an enormous, yellowing, professionally framed, Magic Marker drawing of a swan swimming in a pond of little fish that I made when I was ten. I am waiting for her to get off a conference call so we can go have dinner. For some reason I remember a story she told me about her mother. It turns out that when my mother wasn't away on business trips with my father and a nanny was still looking after me every day, she wasn't shopping as I had always assumed. She was at the library. I asked her years later, "What were you doing there?" "Reading," she said. "Reading what?" I asked. "About computers," she said. When my father died she bought a video camera and a porta-pak and videotaped everything.

My mother was obsessed with the idea of interactive technology. She applied for a grant and went to Reading, Pennsylvania, where she spent time with three groups of elderly people. One group was in a low-income nursing home, one lived in a wealthy retirement community, and the third was in a hospital. They all complained about loneliness and feeling isolated and useless. My mother linked them with videotape and monitors so that they were on a live feed and could communicate. Long before there was an Internet she created one. The seniors made talk shows, they made call-in shows, they made all kinds of programming for themselves. The project was on *60 Minutes*. My mother was on *60 Minutes*. She flew her mother down from Ottawa to see what all the fuss was about and on their way back to the airport my grandmother corrected my mother's driving. My mother said, "Jesus Christ, Ma, I'm fifty-two years old."

My grandmother said, "What do you know? You're just a baby."

I look over at my mother, the big shot. She is holding the receiver in one hand and twirling a chunk of her red hair with the other. I have seen her twirl that chunk of hair a hundred thousand times. It gives me such a feeling of familiarity and comfort. It fills me with love and sheer joy. She smiles at me and makes a face about the person she is talking to on the other end of the phone and I want to crawl into her lap. I am forty-two years old and that is all I ever wanted. It is still what I want.

The sister of the pervert I played with in Aspen died in a fire when I was away at camp two summers later. A boy I loved OD'd when I was twenty-four; my cousin died in childbirth; Rita, the waitress-mentor extraordinaire, hung herself; the girl from Barnard who took

me to Tavern on the Green and started my life as a well-dressed bulimic gassed herself to death in her apartment; my sister's husband
died in broad daylight when he was thirty-nine; now my ex-husband
has cancer. He's not doing well. Death of loved ones runs in my family. I've lost more friends and loved ones than any other ten people I
know put together. My mother is out of town. Out of the country. I
am alone in my living room and she is the only person I want to talk
to. She is almost always the only person I want.

I am asthmatic with her. I can't breathe without her.

It is unbearable. I love her so much.

She must have done something right. What an unsettling thing
to think of so late in life. My mother did something right.

The jitney ride to the Hamptons was very tense because I acciden-
tally left Doll in New York. Olive has never gone anywhere without
Doll. My husband, for some reason, thinks this is not a big deal. He
thinks not having Doll, sleeping without Doll, being separated
from Doll, will be a good experience for Olive. These things build
character, he says. Of course he feels this way—he's not here to see
it unfold. When my mother picks us up at the jitney, we make a
beeline to a toy store to buy a temporary doll. A Hamptons doll.
New Doll has batteries that I promptly removed because had I not,
she would have spoken Hebrew. I almost didn't buy Jewish Doll because the woman in the store didn't feel it was appropriate for
Olive to "handle" the dolls before we bought one. I told her, quite
sharply, that I didn't feel it was appropriate to spend forty-two dollars on a curly haired, Hebrew-speaking doll if my daughter didn't
like cuddling with it. Long story short, Olive and Jewish Doll are
upstairs napping and they seem fine. The phone rings.

"Who was it?" my mother says.

"What?" I shout. "I can't hear you, the TV is so loud. Jesus
Christ."

"I said who was it?"

"Can you turn down the TV? It's like being in an old-age home."

"I can't find the changer. I can't find the remote."

"Of course you can't find the changer. It's so fucking loud in here you can't hear yourself think." That my mother may actually need the television so loud never enters my mind. "You know for someone who runs a department you certainly don't seem to know what you're doing. Here it is." She laughs when I put it in her hand. I love how she can laugh at herself.

"It was my agent. I have a callback for this sitcom tomorrow."

"Well that's good isn't it?"

"Yes, Mother, of course it's good. But I don't feel like getting back on the jitney when Olive wakes up and then dealing with her all day when I should be learning my lines."

"So go back tomorrow?"

"The appointment's too early in the morning and it will screw up her naps and I will be exhausted and I won't know my lines on top of everything else."

"Oh."

"What would you think about me going back tonight? You could put her to bed and I'll be back here tomorrow during her nap." There is no response. "Mom?"

"I don't think I could put her to bed. What if she cries?"

"Are you serious?"

"She cries when you aren't here."

"But you were the one who always told me not to worry when she was crying."

"But it's different now. She can talk."

"Exactly. I'll explain it to her. I can even put her to bed and leave after that. I'll learn my lines on the bus and then go to the ap-pointment and come back tomorrow." There is still no response. "Mom?" I ask her again. "I won't feel comfortable," she answers. I can't believe how completely unhelpful my mother is. I am furious.

I watch her go up the stairs gripping the railing for support. And then I see that she is scared to be left with her. To walk up to the third floor in the middle of night if Olive needs something. Of carrying her, of lifting her into her crib, of being alone with her in case something happened. To either of them.

Olive screams bloody murder every time she has to make a poopy. She runs around in circles screaming and crying and hiding behind furniture and then demanding to sit on my lap where she tries as hard as she can either to hold it in or let it out. I can't tell which. There are people coming over for dinner. People I don't know very well. People in fact I have never met before. They are friends of my husband. I was hoping she would be in bed by the time they came over, but the timing didn't work out. When they arrive Olive is not trying to make a poopy so she's really friendly.

"Well I go to school," she tells them with happy authority. "What's your mom's name?" she asks the woman guest after being introduced. She shows everyone her Polly Pockets. She is charming. She is outgoing. She is an utter delight. But when dinner is ready my pride turns to embarrassment. Olive won't join us at the table. It is time to poop. She is screaming and running in circles and hiding and needing to sit on my lap. I know what the people are thinking. They don't have kids, and this is why. She is acting like a spoiled brat. I can see that. The people are nice. They pretend her crying and whining is not annoying and that I am a fine mother. They are good natured and ignore the fact that she is talking about her bowels in graphic detail while they are eating their dinner. She is sitting in my lap at the dinner table screaming and crying, "My poopy, Mom! Aaahhh. It's not coming out. Help me!" Everyone present, including the father of my child, thinks I have crossed the line from good parenting to complete indulgence. I am beginning to wonder myself. But I believe her. If she says she's in pain she's in pain. Although it is a little suspicious that the pain started precisely when the adults were called to a piping hot dinner that I spent all day cooking.

"Olive," the woman says, trying to engage her after an awkward lull.

"I'm trying a make a poopy," Olive says by way of response.

"Oh," the woman says.

"I are it's not coming out. Mommmy! I are having trouble. Aahhhhhhhhh!"

"She's constipated," I explain. My husband gives me a dirty look.

"Oh," the woman says but isn't sure what to say next. She is from the Midwest and met the man she's with a few months ago. According to him he had a good feeling about her and told her they should just get married. So she left cheese country two weeks ago and moved in with him. This is her first dinner out with friends. "I think I was like that too," she tells Olive. "I think my parents gave me prune juice." She's very sweet.

"I *do* have prune juice. But it's *not* working," Olive says, pouring her heart out.

"Oh," the woman says.

"Aaaaahhh. I need a get down." Olive yells at me like I am making it worse and bolts off my lap. She runs around in circles screaming. Dinner's going really well. "Help me!" she screams. "Aaaahhh I need a sit in your lap." She climbs back in my lap and then screams at the top of her lungs, *"I made a poopy! Change my diaper!"* I really have no idea where the line between indulgence and love lies. I really don't. I'm a total amateur.

Olive's school (that is not Friends) puts a lot of stock in "the power of communication." Me too. I have to since I think everything wrong with the world is based on a misunderstanding of some sort or another and if the parties involved could just talk about it the world would be a better place.

On Olive's first day, I am disappointed with her teachers. I want teachers who are loving and nurturing or dynamic and inspiring. Ideally, these four qualities would appear in one person, but I will settle for one set in each person. She has one teacher who is warmth personified. I am satisfied with her. The other one is a coraller; all I see her doing is enforcing the rules, which all seem idiotic. Crisscross applesauce, stand on the blue line, choice time—I find the rules and the schedule overwhelming and I am not three, I am forty. On Olive's third day of school, I told her I would be outside in the hall if she needed me, which is the first step toward leaving the building. After about ten minutes I heard her start to cry and say she wanted me. But the teacher did not say, "Okay, she's right outside like she told you she'd be." She said sternly, "Olive, no one else has their mother in here. Mommies are gone. This is school time not Mommy time." Well I walked right through the door, furious, and said, "Hi, lovey, how's it going?" No one is going to break a promise I made to my child. I said I would be right outside the door if she needed me and that's that.

I am also mad because I don't understand why they haven't taken a minute to explain the fascist schedule. Every minute of their time is accounted for and I think that is a big concept for three-year-olds, who have been free agents their whole lives, to get their minds around. On the way to school the next day I do the teachers' job for them. I review with Olive what will happen so she will know what to expect and feel secure. In the four days there they have never, as a class, talked about the schedule. I say, "So Olive honey, first when we get there it will be roof time, and then it will be snack time, and then it's circle time. Does that sound good?" She interrupts me, "No. First it's roof time, and then it's circle time, and *then* it's snack time." In the classroom they have added a wheel with photographs of all the activities of the day arranged in order.

Bravo, I think. Finally, a visual reference so the kids know what's coming next. Except, as Olive pointed out to me, they don't need it. They figured it out three days ago.

Olive and I are going to a gastroenterologist referred by her pediatrician. She's been taking five tablespoons of mineral oil a day for three months and she's still constipated. Oil squirts out of her ass but she can't make a poopy for days at a time and then when she finally does, it is so enormous, it is no wonder she screams in pain. Waiting for the train, people give me the evil eye.

"I am having trouble making a poopy," she tells the people on the platform. She tells the people inside the subway, "I can't make a poopy." "My poopy is stuck," she tells the people in the bus across town. Her specialist is on the Upper East Side. That's what I want in a specialist. I grilled the receptionist on the phone before I made the appointment.

"Is he a nice man?" I asked.

"Oh yes, Dr. Spillman is a very nice man," Amy assured me. "He's very conservative and he won't recommend anything drastic. He's a very wait-and-see kind of man."

"All right, as long as he's nice," I warn her. "And gentle."

The doctor appears and says, "You must be Olive."

"I are having trouble making a poopy," she tells him.

His examination room is nice. There is a Snoopy poster circa 1972. He makes Olive count how many Woodstocks there are.

"Free," she tells him. He ignores her and interrogates me: her diet, allergies, her delivery, when did the problem start, when was her last bowel movement. Olive wants to talk too.

"Well. I drink mineroil," she interjects, but he is not interested.

"Is she toilet trained?" he asks me instead.

"She uses the potty and she uses diapers."

"She's not toilet trained then?"

"She uses the potty and she uses diapers," I repeat. She's a little bit toilet trained. She's working on it. She has an interest in the toilet, but she's not exclusive about it and I am not the type to remove her diapers, like Jack's mother, and then deride her when she goes on the floor, like Jack's mother did to Jack.

"Okay," Dr. Spillman says, like Olive is a car in a garage. "Let's get her on the table. Sit up here, cutie." The cutie part is an afterthought. He reminds me of the French Israeli OB I went to once when I was pregnant. He addressed my entire examination to Adam, even though I was the one with the baby inside and the one whose vagina he was twirling the ultrasound penis around in. Rude.

"Who told you there were fissures?" he asks, spreading Olive's legs.

"Her pediatrician. We saw them yesterday."

"Well there are none there," he says closing Olive's legs. Olive wants to pee. He tells me to give her a diaper. I do. She pees. I ask him if I should throw it in the garbage can. "No. I will give you a bag to dispose of it." He never does.

"All right," he says with dread after Olive is dressed and I have returned to his desk. I am still holding her wet diaper in my hand. "Who lives at home?"

"Her father and I."

"Oh, I saw the two different names," he says, relieved, as though the diagnosis will be easier now. "There is nothing wrong with her," he continues. "She is just constipated, which is fairly common, and her colon has stretched. I want you to give her Senocot for two weeks, and she needs to be toilet trained. I want her to sit on the potty with her feet firmly touching the ground three times a day after meals for ten minutes. Make a chart and reward her with stickers and rewards for each bowel movement that goes in the potty. And you will come back in two weeks and show me the chart."

"She's not toilet trained—" I start to say.

"She needs to be," he interrupts me again. "That is part of the problem."

"You know she's a smart girl and my philosophy is that when she's ready—" he interrupts me again.

"It's time for her to be potty trained. She is much too backed up and the urge to go is confused now because her colon has stretched. The Senocot will not only give her the urge to go, but the urge will be followed by relief and the bad association with going to the bathroom will be replaced by relief."

"I understand that, but she doesn't like to poop on the potty. Can she do it in a diaper but sitting on the potty?"

"No. If you follow *these* instructions—Senocot, potty time *three* times a day for ten minutes, and a system of rewards and stickers—the problem will be fixed. Do you want the problem fixed? I assume that is why you came to see me."

"Yes, but I don't really go for forcing her to do things she might not be ready for." I hate him. He obviously doesn't have children and if he does, he doesn't spend any time with them.

"Bring the chart in two weeks. I want to see it. Children her age respond very well to stickers and rewards." He stands up. Apparently he is finished with us. He hands me the photocopied instruction sheet. I look at his hands. No wedding ring. This is the last time I take Olive to a doctor without children. They haven't got a clue.

As I pay, Amy asks, "How did it go? Did you like Dr. Spillman? He's a nice man."

"He doesn't have children, does he?"

"What makes you say that?"

"He wasn't wearing a wedding ring," I say.

"No. He doesn't wear a wedding ring, but he's married. He has three children."

"Really?"

"Yes, really."

"You're sure? I thought maybe he didn't."

"No, he does and he's married. What made you say something about the ring?"

"I don't know. I just try and make it a practice to bring Olive to doctors with children of their own. I find their advice easier to follow."

"He doesn't wear a ring because his *wife* wants him to."

"Oh," I say, not sure how to respond to this seemingly personal information.

"He doesn't wear a ring. But he is definitely married. See those three children in the picture over there? They are his children." I look at the poster-size blow-up of three smiling blond girls.

"Oh," I say again.

"Yes," she says. "And I am his wife."

"Oh," I say.

"We have been married for thirty years. He doesn't wear a ring." Dr. Spillman comes out of his office.

"Amy, I need the Gabriel chart," he announces.

"Yes, Dr. Spillman," she says.

If I had to work with my husband every day, and not even with him, but *for* him, I would have to be medicated at best. My mother always implied that if my father hadn't died they would have been divorced by now. She says he wanted to move to a retirement community where he could play golf in the sun all day. They were married for eleven years. She could stand that, but the golf and the sun would have been a deal breaker. I'd rather move to a retirement community with nice appliances than work for my husband every day and call him "Dr. Forgash."

I am four. My mother and I are at the doctor's office for the hundredth time this winter. I am always sick. My doctor is married to the receptionist. She calls him "Dr. Smith." My mother says the reason she does is because Dr. Smith is "just ridiculous and very rigid." Then she tells me that it is bad to be rigid and to talk with a New York accent and to be a nervous driver. She also tells me I am going to get a tonsillectomy. Dr. Smith thinks it is a good idea. Everybody's doing it and getting sick less. In the taxi down Lexington Avenue she says, "It's not going to hurt because you won't feel a thing. They're going to knock you out."

"What?" I say, terrified.

"I mean they are going to knock you out. You will be under anesthesia. You won't feel a thing. You will be asleep, and when you wake up it will be over."

"Where are my tonsils?"

"Over here," she says, gesturing vaguely at her throat, chest, and both of her shoulders.

"What are they?"

"I have no idea, but it doesn't matter, because whatever they are, they're clearly not very important since you won't miss them when they're gone."

"How long will I be in the hopsital?" (The word "hospital" is very tricky. Half the time I think I'm saying it wrong and the rest of the time I'm sure I'm saying it wrong.)

"A couple of days."

"Will you visit me?"

"Visit you? Are you crazy? I'm not leaving you. You are not spending the night in a hospital without your mother. We're going to a special hospital where mothers sleep too. I insisted on it. They're going to bring in a bed for me. You'll see."

At the hospital they never bring my mother a bed and they take my clothes away. It's unnerving. They replace my going-to-the-hospital outfit, which I worked very hard to pick out, with a weird navy blue and white nightgown that has no back and no matter what position I am in my left foot ends up in the right armhole. My mother spends the night in her clothes in the chair next to my bed. In the morning a person takes me away to get the operation. My mother clutches her heart with one hand and waves goodbye with the other, like she is saying goodbye to her lover at the train in a black-and-white war picture with steam billowing up all around us. I watch her get smaller and smaller until she disappears completely. She was wearing black from head to toe and carrying my favorite purse before she disappeared. The one with the big gold *H* on the front that makes the clicking sound when you open and shut it. As my gurney and I turn a corner I yell for her to be there when I get back. But I'm sure she can't hear me.

I wake up without my tonsils and a raging sore throat in a room filled with other children waking up from surgery. There are balloons everywhere. My mother would never bring me a balloon, I think. It's hard to have a mother who doesn't believe in balloons and is older than other mothers and who yells at you when you make her a menu for Mother's Day with carefully drawn pictures of the foods you know how to make for her breakfast because, according to her, your family doesn't believe in Mother's Day because it's just a commercial bunch of Hallmark crap.

I look at the other kids in the recovery room. Everyone is dazed and frightened. I wonder if that's what I look like. And then I take a closer look. It's so sad. No one's mother is there. Except mine. It is absolutely incredible. I am the only child in that room, maybe in that hospital, whose mother came back on time. The only one. Tears fall down from my eyes. I believe in God, in magic, luck— anything—everything —who cares. My mother says, "Of course I was back in time. They told me you would be done at eleven and I made sure to be back at ten. They don't always happen to know what they're talking about. I wanted to be the first thing you saw when you opened your eyes." She says this to me as though I am a dummy. And I was. I never thought she would be there.

MIND THE GAP

I've resorted to stickers and prizes. I will never tell Dr. Spillman any of this, but Olive gets a Swedish Fish for pooping, period—in her diaper, in her bed, on the potty, anywhere—and she gets a present if she does it on the potty without her diaper. The candy is bad for her teeth and it isn't really working anyway. She hasn't pooped for six days. It's time to pull out the big gun. Lisa Lillienfeld. She costs two hundred dollars an hour but she's always right. She thinks Spillman is a genius and she wants his number. I give it to her but I tell her he's an asshole. She says an asshole is better than a nice guy who prescribes enemas. She tells me I have to potty train Olive.

"The longer kids go, the harder it is for them to do it. I think Olive needs you to help her get to the next level. Take away her diapers and make a weekend project out of it, stop with the presents, and just do it. Tell her you have complete confidence in her. I really think the whole thing will be resolved when she gets out of diapers."

"Really?"

"I really do. I think she's just having trouble going there on her own so you have to help her."

That night, after her bath, I tell her that tomorrow we're going to do a project. No diapers all day and we're going to work on using the potty. She seems excited about the plan and even reports it to Adam like it is wonderful news. We cancel all our plans for the weekend so we can stay inside and potty train.

In the morning I take off her wet diaper and when I don't put on another one she freaks out. She starts kicking and screaming and climbs down and gets a diaper from the shelf and tries to put it on herself. She begs for a diaper.

"Honey, remember what we talked about last night? We're not using a diaper today. You're going to use the potty whenever you need to make a pee or a poopy."

"*Nooooooo!* I want my diaper. I want my diaper."

"Lovey just for today, okay? We'll see how it goes. We really think you're ready and can I tell you something? I would never ever ask you to do something if I didn't think you were ready."

"No. I want a diaper. I want a diaper! I want a diaper!" She is working herself up into a major lather.

"What are you afraid of, honey? You already use the potty sometimes, we're just trying to get you to use it even more."

Through her tears she says, "I'm not ready. I'm not *ready*!"

"Olive, honey, everyone thinks this is going to help you with your poopy trouble and we're going to try it and see how it works. I know you can do it. I promise you you can do it."

"No I can't!" she cries. Finally she lets go of the diaper and she cries in my arms. After breakfast she announces she needs to pee and she does. She keeps telling us what happened, "I peed in the potty." She is very proud. Then she needs to poop. So she does. And she poops five more times, in the potty, before the day is done. It's done and she's cured. All they need is a little help. All I need is to act like I know how to help her. It's a confidence game, a charade.

Olive told me this morning she will not eat a peanut butter and jam sandwich if I put it in her lunch box. She didn't say no tortellini so I am standing in the kitchen like my mother before me, making noodles for my emaciated child to bring to school for lunch. She hasn't eaten anything for five days; what choice do I have? She hasn't pooped either, but I don't want to think about that. So I won't. Even though it's obvious she's holding it in again. Every time she gets sick, she regresses with pooping. When I take the tortellini out of the freezer there are only five left in the bag.

"Olive there aren't enough tortellini, so I'm making you gnocchi."

"*No*. I *want* tortellini. I don't want *gnocchi*." I am about to remind her that I am in charge but I put on another pot of water instead. Then I tell myself that I have nothing to worry about, she's not bossing me around. I have a handle on the situation. I'm *still* making her the gnocchi. I'm just making both. The tortellini and the gnocchi.

"Olive, I am making you the gnocchi. You can eat the tortellini first and if you're still hungry you will eat the gnocchi." I have two pots on the stove. No, three pots, two for pasta, one for parboiled carrots (because my Chinese doctor thinks cooked carrots are better for small developing digestive systems), no, four pots because I am also making oatmeal for her breakfast. I can barely see through the steam. I linger in it, letting it collect on my face because it's good for my skin and it's the closest I'm going to come to a facial anytime soon.

"Olive, drink your milk please."

"No."

"Olive, drink your milk. If you won't eat you have to drink. It is my job to make sure you get nourishment. I can't help it."

"I don't want to," she says. "My tummy and my tushie hurt."

"Olive, do you have to make a poopy?"

"No. Ow."

"Olive, are you holding your poopy in? You know you'll feel better as soon as you let it out."

"No."

"Let it out!"

"No!"

"Olive, I don't want to hear it. Drink your milk or you are going back in your bed." I am practicing being tough because the more liquids she takes, the easier it will be for her to poop. Plus, last night my husband gave me a silent lecture, with his eyes, during dinner, about how she walks all over me. He thinks she's not eating to bug me. He probably thinks she's holding her bowels to bug me.

She drinks her milk and shows me the cup. There is a little left at the bottom. I make her finish it even though she doesn't want to just to prove to my husband, who isn't even in the room, that his daughter doesn't walk all over me, that I'm the boss.

"My tushy and my tummy hurt too much," she whines.

"Olive, please don't whine. If you have something to say just say it. Talk like a normal person. I can't listen to the whining."

"Ow. My throat hurts," she whimpers.

"What do you mean your throat hurts?" My patience is shot. She holds in her poopy until she gets a gut-wrenching stomachache. And the day she finally relents and does go, the potty is literally full to the top with the poop that has been lodged inside her until she can barely walk. She holds it in until she is in more pain than I can comfortably handle without getting mad or scared or emotional, which I am not supposed to do, because I have been instructed that the correct response is to say very calmly, "When you are ready you will make a poopy and you will feel better." It's beyond driving me crazy. I can't take it anymore. Between the whining, the complaints, the orders, the never doing what I ask without an argument . . . I am so fed up I can't stand it. I want to go away, anywhere I can be alone, and where my only responsibility is choosing what kind of juice to have in the morning. My daydream of juice and solitude is yanked away when I hear the sound of Olive vomiting all over the floor.

She shrieks, shocked and impressed at the giant puddle of throw up spreading out on the floor in front of her.

"Oh my God, Olive, honey are you all right?" I feel awful. It's my fault. She shouldn't have drunk all that milk. She was listening to her body, and I was listening to my ego and I bossed her around so she would know I was in charge.

"I'm sick," she says. My heart breaks. "Clean it up," she barks. I get the mop.

But I want to break it over her head.

My mother calls. "I thought of you today," she says. "I saw a little person, a girl no more than Olive's age, sitting down on the side-walk, not moving, like you used to do. Do you remember? You used to get so mad you would turn blue. I saw her mother leaning over her saying, 'I don't understand. Do you want to walk down Fifth Avenue or Sixth Avenue?' 'Fifth Avenue,' the little girl said. And it so reminded me of you. How is Olive?"

"She's fine except she hasn't crapped for five days. I guess I have to give her laxatives again. But, can I just ask you, what kind of person only eats carrot sticks and apples, and takes laxatives and is obsessed with ballet?" My mother is not amused. I find it very amusing, in a New Yorker cover sort of way, that I have a three-year-old pseudoanorexic.

"Maybe you should go back to that doctor."

"I hate that doctor."

"There are other doctors. Why don't you go to the one you liked so much when you thought she was having seizures?"

"The neurologist?"

"The one who told you it was only breath-holding."

"Because he's a neurologist. This is not a neurological problem. If I should go to anyone it's a psychiatrist. She likes to hold everything in, her breath, her bowels—you know her first sentence was 'I don't want to talk about it.' It's all about control."

"That doesn't make any sense."

"Why?"

"Mommy?" Olive says.

"Olive, honey, I'm on the phone."

"I don't know. It just doesn't," my mother says.

"It does to me."

"Mommy. Peter Pan's foots are bigger in this picture than in this picture." Olive holds up the box from the Peter Pan movie and compares it to the far superior J. M. Barrie book.

"Olive, I'm on the phone. Show me after, okay?"

"I take those Chinese herbs now and my stool is soft and it comes out like clockwork every morning."

"I know, Mother. So far you told me that twice this week, but hers is soft. She just likes to push it back in. Before she was potty trained and cured, I saw her do it. She went six days without going and it was finally coming out and she squeezed it back in, I saw it disappear right in front of my eyes. I thought I was going to kill myself."

"Mommy," Olive says again.

"She's on the phone, Ollie!" my husband yells from the other room.

"But she seems in pain," my mother continues.

"I know but I think she's screaming because it is actually coming out and she wants to push it back in. That's why that doctor put her on the laxatives so she would be forced to let it out and then get used to letting it out. Which is what happened. She was totally regular for three months until she got sick at Christmas and she went a little backward."

"That doesn't make any sense."

"Well it does to me. He said he had never seen a child take that much laxative and still manage to hold it in. He said she had uncharted control."

"Mommy."

"Olive, can you see I am on the phone?"

"No," she says looking at me holding the phone against my ear.

"*Olive!*" I move about one inch away from her face. "Now can you see I am on the phone?"

"No," she says with a big flirtatious smile. She's trying to bug me. She is so annoying and it's a skill I share so I can't help but admire her talents. I did it to my mother all the time. Now I do it to my husband. I bug him until he laughs with pure adoration or he gets so mad I have to stop immediately and run out of the room. She's my little acorn and she didn't fall far from the tree.

"I guess you'll see what happens. I'll tell you the one thing no one told me that I wish they had. Keep your sense of humor. I took all these things very seriously." I tell my mother how I got tough with Olive and made her drink all her milk and then she threw up. My mother says, "Oh no! She was sick. Poor thing."

"That's what I thought and I felt so bad about it because it is an amazing thing to know your own body and so few people really do and I was berating myself for cracking down when all of a sudden she instructed me to '*clean* it up.' Like I am her servant. Like I am the maid." My mother starts choking she's laughing so much.

"Well that's what they do, they test you and they want to be independent and they push you and they drive you crazy and I've got news for you. It just gets worse."

"Oh great."

"But then it gets better. And then it gets worse. But it does get better."

"Do you really think so?" I say. I am totally fishing for compliments.

"Jesus, don't you? I'm living proof. Listen, it's very hard. Children want to find their own way, they want to test things out, they want to explore, they want to be independent, and their parents want them to behave and occasionally children say, 'Go fuck yourself,' and that's not a bad thing. You used to scream until you turned blue in the face and I would be terrified you were going to die of asphyxiation. I had no sense of humor at all. The fact is, it's all supposition. Nobody knows what anybody else is doing or thinking. That doctor doesn't know what's going on in Olive's head. Nobody knows anything. And the fact is it is very hard to live with other people."

"Mommy," Olive says smiling at me. She knows she is dangerously close to no longer being a cute pest, but a really annoying one.

"Olive," I say on the verge of laughing.

"Go be with your daughter," my mother instructs and hangs up so she can spend the rest of the day alone.

What a cruel twist of fate, I think, that I waited so long to have a child. My mother won't be here when Olive is a teenager and every interaction between us is fraught with tension and contempt. Who will I talk to? Maybe I deserve to be alone then. Perfect payback for being a contempt-filled adolescent myself for fifteen years too many.

I am racing. I have to get back to Brooklyn from my audition in the city to pick Olive up at the school (that is not Friends) and get her back to the city where I will drop her off at the PATH station so my husband can take her to New Jersey where his father will pick her up and take her home with him for the weekend. It is snowing like crazy. When I get to her classroom the teachers tell me Olive already explained to them she wasn't staying for lunch today because she was going to her grandma's house. We get all our stuff and Olive tells everyone again, "I have to leave. I am going to my gaga's house." It is very tricky getting into the subway. There is already a foot of snow. I don't think I can carry her and the stroller down the stairs without killing at least one of us.

"Olive, honey, this is the plan—" I begin.

"What?" she interrupts, ready for anything.

"I'm going to walk with you down the stairs and then you're going to wait there while I go back up to get the stroller. And we'll keep doing that until we get to the bottom. Okay? It's really slippy, so be careful. Okay?"

"Okay," she says, and we start our descent down the first of three ice-covered staircases. When we get to the bottom of the first one I tell her to wait right there while I get the stroller. I see us sort of playing leapfrog like this down the stairs and am reminded of a book we read about a chicken named Lottie. Lottie is trying to get to the water to meet her duck friend Herbie for a picnic. But the hot sand is burning her toes. So she jumps on top of her cooler to get some relief. Then she throws her beach towel out in front of the cooler and jumps on it. Now she has a system. She makes her way down to the beach jumping from her towel onto her cooler over and over until she reaches Herbie. It's obviously a little bit different for me and Olive right now, because it's winter and we're not chickens and there's no towel, but still. I get to the bottom of the stairs lugging the stroller and Olive is on her way back up.

"What are you doing, lovey?" I ask her.

"I'm coming back to get you," she says smiling at me.

On the subway I ponder my impending freedom. While Olive is in New Jersey I will go to the movies with my husband. I will have sex with my husband, I hope. Unless the pressure of doing it because we're finally alone is too much for us, which it usually is, so we don't. I am so excited. Even though I know myself. When I get home I will look at her empty bed, touch her cold pajamas, refold all her clothes a hundred times, and ache for her.

"I love you, Olive. I'm going to miss you."

"Why?"

"Because you will be with Gaga and Noonoo until I see you at Rose's birthday party on Sunday." Sometimes I feel like Olive is a little briefcase full of money that keeps changing hands in a heist. "Will you call me anytime you feel like it?"

"Yes I will," she tells me. "And I will always keep loving you."

"Well, me too."

At Chambers Street I kiss my husband hello and goodbye and kiss Olive goodbye.

"Where are you going?" she asks.

"I'm going home, honey, and Daddy's taking you on the train to meet Noonoo."

"Is he coming with me to Gaga's?"

"No, honey," he says. "I'm bringing you to Noonoo, who's taking you to Gaga's."

She knew she was going to New Jersey for the weekend to be with Gramma and Grampa, but maybe I didn't explain all the little intricacies of the plan enough for her. I leave in a panic. On the subway home I think about how lucky I am, to have her, to have in-laws who are thrilled to have her for the weekend, to have a husband, to have something I love to do—like write. I am literally counting my blessings, all four of them, and promising myself to treat her with more care and respect when a stranger interrupts me.

"Is this the C?" the man says.

"Yes," I say.

"Thank you. God bless you."

"No problem," I say a little surprised at the fervor of his reply. He sits down next to me and unfolds a copy of the *Daily News*. He shakes the paper at me and asks, "Did you see this? A little boy was run over in front of his own mother. I can't read it. I can't look at it." He closes the paper. I catch a glimpse of the story before he does. It is gruesome. A mother was holding hands with her son, walking him to school, when a car, driven by another mother, lost control and flung the little boy out of his mother's grip and pinned him between the car and a tree and he died instantly. "People don't know what they have. You know? This one's mad because he don't have sneakers, this one's complaining because she's late. Nobody knows nothing. Count your blessings. You know?"

"Amen," I say. I get off at Jay Street–Borough Hall to change for the F and it pulls away as I approach the platform.

"Fuck," I mutter. Then I remember what he said. So I say a little prayer for everyone who lost someone and walk home in the snow. The streets of Brooklyn are quiet and ethereal. The branches of the trees are double dipped, thick and white. Everything I pass looks like a giant snowflake. The world is magnificent. Life is for the living. I go home and call Olive.

Mary-Kate doesn't like dance class. She keeps coming out, looking for her father.

"Why are you out here?" he says coldly. "All the big girls are in there. Dancing like *big* girls. You're going to have a sister. You have to be a big girl. Go. Back. In." There is no affection in his voice. Mary-Kate clings and cries, but her appeal goes nowhere so she finally gives up. She hangs her head and goes back in. Her father rolls his eyes at me.

"She's so dramatic," he says thinking he will get sympathy from me. He picked the wrong person.

"Maybe she just misses you," I say.

"No. She's just being dramatic. She does the same thing when we leave her at school."

"Maybe she misses you at school."

"No. There's no reason for that. She's been there since she was two."

"Well it might be true anyway," I say.

"It's time for her to leave the nest," he says.

"Jeez, she's only three. She has the rest of her life not to like you."

"I can't wait. When will that start?"

I hate that this guy is having another baby. Why do people have more children if the ones they already have are such a nuisance to them?

"What school did you end up at?" he asks me. I try to place him. He reminds me, we were on the same Friends tour two years ago.

"Open House," I say. "What about you?"

"Friends," he says.

I can't believe this asshole got into Friends.

Olive and I are applying again. I can't help it. I am determined. Part of my attraction to Friends is that even though it is a private school, its location in downtown Brooklyn makes it seem gritty and not precious, as though it were actually part of the real world. I look at Olive in her stroller. She's such a trouper. After our interview we're going to have a ladies' date and get hot chocolate and a treat. She is three years old and instead of letting her take a well-deserved and necessary nap, I'm making her wow the people at Friends. The whole thing is so ridiculous.

It is windy and raining ice. I am wrestling with my umbrella, which keeps turning inside out. I'm getting clobbered because holding an umbrella over my own head with one hand and steering the stroller in and out of ravines of slush with the other is impossible. Especially for my five-foot-two frame, which hasn't exercised in four years. This winter is relentless. I'm over it. And we're lost.

I ask Innocent Bystander Number Three where Pearl Street is. Everyone thinks it's right here somewhere, but they don't know where exactly. I am so grateful for the plastic rain shield on the stroller because I think it is protecting Olive from grasping the gravity of our situation, that I am a useless mother and that we might be late for her entire future. I am now asking a cop. He doesn't know where it is either. Of course not. Pearl Street is only two blocks long and the only people who know where it is are rich, white, homogenized assholes who can afford to send their kids to Friends.

We get there with seconds to spare. I check out the competition. One boy is sucking on a pacifier. *We can take him out*, I assure myself. His mother looks like a fire hydrant, low and squat, dressed in a red power suit. Everyone begins moving toward the fantastic gold filigreed elevator that will take us upstairs for our interviews. As we're getting into the elevator, the fire hydrant hisses, "Give me the pacifier!" and she stuffs it in her purse.

Riding in the elevator I can feel the giggles and growing pains of thousands of children imbedded in the layers of paint on the walls. The elevator operator looks like he loves his job and being around children all day. He seems like a gentle old soul. He reminds me of Charlie the elevator man from Park Avenue. I bet this guy would look out for Olive the way Charlie looked out for me.

Upstairs the children are steered into a classroom to play with teachers and the parents are sent around the corner. Olive gets to play while she is being judged and I get to interview while I am judged. I can't wait for the hot chocolate. The fire hydrant maneuvers her way to being interviewed first. Through the closed door I can hear her bragging her way into placement next year. "He knows many four- and five-syllable words," she says. *Big fucking deal*, I think. I sound out pacifier in my head. *Pa-ci-fi-er*. I imagine knocking on the door and sticking my head in, "Yoo-hoo. Pacifier! That's a four-syllable word, you asshole." But I don't. They'll probably get in.

When it is my turn I tell the truth. That Olive is shy. That she prefers adults. That she is goofy and hilarious and witty and outgoing at home or with me or her dad. But at school she is cautious and that they recommended she have more playdates. I tell them that she is exceptionally verbal, but a little clumsy on her feet. I tell them that philosophically I believe in public school but that the dumb No Child Left Behind bill makes school's primary concern be test scores. If teachers can light kids' imaginations on fire while preparing them for the tests, great, but that's not their job. I tell them that I went to a private school very much like Friends. That I loved school as a child, and that my husband who went to public school did not. That he is more polite than me, but that I have never doubted my mind or that I could do anything I wanted. I tell them I am grateful to my school. It allowed me to learn in an environment that encouraged growth. My ideas got bigger, my imagination got bigger, I got bigger. I tell them that is what I want for Olive. And then we're done. But I don't brag. I don't tell hilarious anecdotes about her. I don't sell her. I won't do that. Any school that gets her will be lucky to have her. They would be honored to have her in their building, creating a life inside their walls, contributing to their world.

Olive watches from a bench in the park. The other kids tear the place up, running around while she watches. Sometimes she draws. But if we stay more than an hour she starts to get involved. It is painful to see your child on the outside. Although, who am I to say, maybe she enjoys her sociological perspective. At school her day starts on the roof. We climb up the stairs singing the "we are marching to the roof" song and she is genuinely excited. But when we get to the roof, she just watches as the other kids chase each other. I tell myself that Olive's strong suit has never been running and jumping. If her day started inside, with puzzles and arts and crafts, maybe she would dive right in. There's one boy, Truman, who always wears his Bob the Builder outfit and stands in the pretend kitchen cooking. All morning he makes breakfast out of blocks and hammers and serves it up.

It takes Olive a long time to absorb all the action. I stay until she says that it's okay for me to leave. Sometimes I try and jump-start her. I put her on the seesaw with someone, start climbing in the weird cube thing that is part hideout and part jungle gym. "Come on Libby!" I say to one of the kids who's been in day care since she was three months old. She's totally used to being left. "Nice new coat, Violet. Fancy," I say to Violet, Olive's friend, whose mother disappears every morning without saying goodbye while Violet's not looking. "Olive, look at Vi's new coat. Isn't it nice?" As soon as they all start playing I say bye again and leave. Maybe I should just let her find her own way. I'm not going to be there for-ever to help her. What is my responsibility exactly? How on earth do you love someone without either smothering them or con-stantly letting them down?

"There is a real girl in my dance class who is the same name as Madeline," Olive told me 150 times this week, and she just re-minded me again as we are on our way out the door to ballet.

At ballet I get her dressed, pat her on the tutu, and kiss her goodbye. I wait outside, like I'm supposed to. I am not allowed to watch my adorable little creation parade around in her ballet out-fit. They don't even have a window to peep through, that's how serious Frances, the owner, is. No watching. Ballet is not for the weak at heart, the sentimental. It's for toughies. I hate it. But I don't mess with Frances, who walks around with a big stick poking mothers who are trying to listen through the closed door. Read-ing a magazine, I watch a mom drag her sobbing, hyperventilating child by the wrist up the stairs. The kid is upset, probably because she can't keep up and because she suspects her arm is about to pop out of its socket. There is no tenderness when you drag a child by the wrist. I hate people who don't hold their kid's hand. At the top of the stairs the mom starts ripping the girl's snowsuit off until a little pink ballerina outfit is revealed underneath. The little girl doesn't want to go to class.

"Madeline, are you being a baby?" she asks her daughter.

Ohmigod it's Madeline! I want to run in and tell Olive, "Madeline is here! I saw the real Madeline!" Since I am not allowed in and Frances is still roaming the halls I want to tell Madeline herself how much I have been hearing about her. But I realize this is probably not a good time. Madeline is clinging to her mother. Her mother is peeling her off like a leech.

"What? You don't want to be a big girl? You want to be a *baby* and stay at home with a babysitter?"

"*No!*" Madeline sobs.

"No, what?" her mother says. I want to pick Madeline up in my arms.

"What, Madeline. Should I go get my money back? You don't want to dance like Zooey?"

"I want my daddy," Madeline cries.

"All right, that's it! I'm getting my money back and you are staying at home and that's the end of classes for you. I'm not fighting with you. Come on!" She starts shoving Madeline back into her parka and her winter boots and her gloves and her hat. She grabs her by the wrist again and drags her downstairs. She's walking too fast and Madeline can't keep up, especially in her all her winter clothes. I am so furious at Madeline's mother, I can barely contain myself. Her mother, totally frustrated by how slow Madeline is, finally picks her up sideways and carries her downstairs. She picks Madeline up like she is a big fat pain in the ass.

Every summer the grandchildren converge at my mother's for a few weeks. It is the highlight of the year for me. I love my nieces so much and I love seeing them with Olive.

"Are you done with the newspaper?" my mother barks at me in the morning. She pulls the Metro section away from the table.

"No. I'm still reading it. Can I have it back?" My mother ignores me and walks out of the room. "Wait, I'm going to read that part next. Did you actually throw it away already?"

"Yes I did. You are too slow. I want to go to the dump. Are you finished with the coffee?"

"I don't know yet, I'm still drinking this cup. Do I have to decide now?" She's already out of her mind and we only got here yesterday. I hate it when my mother is this nervous. Someone is going to get hurt. Yesterday she whacked herself in the head with her car door. She drew blood. When she's nervous she does everything too fast. I must remember to try not to drive with her anywhere.

"This kitchen is a mess," she says to no one in particular. "Whose pan is this? I don't like the milk cartons on the table. Is Olive finished with this? What is this? Oatmeal? Can I throw it out? I can't stand the waste. Is it possible for anyone in this house to leave the kitchen as they found it?"

"Red, for Christ's sake, would you slow down," my brother says.

"Don't tell me to slow down. This is my house. It is not your house. Why are there so many towels out?" My brother and his very good-looking wife roll their eyes. Olive and her cousins appear on the landing and turn right around at the mention of the towels. *The towels the towels the towels.* This will go down in history as the summer of the towels.

"Oh my God, Mom. There are three children here. The house is fine. It just looks like there are kids here," I say.

"I'm going for a walk on the beach," she announces to the sink. The screen door slams behind her. "Daisy and Sally, hang up the towels. Bubbe Red is on the warpath," my brother yells up the stairs.

"I'm busy," Sally answers back. Why should a seven-year-old stop watching *SpongeBob SquarePants* and put down sugar-frosted cereal to clean up? Why should I clean out the coffeepot before

I've enjoyed my first actual cup? No one knows the answer to these things.

"I'm not coming next year!" my sister-in-law yells at my brother.

"She's gone a little batty," my brother says about our mother.

"She's always a little batty," my sister-in-law says. "And if I hear one more thing about the *fucking towels* I'm leaving. That's it. I am taking the girls with me and we're leaving. We are on vacation and we will use as many towels as we want."

"All right, all right," my brother says. My brother really thinks that all that's wrong with our mother is that she lives alone. "She doesn't have anyone around to tell her when she's being crazy. Everyone needs someone around to tell them they've gone too far." Anyone can see that. But can anyone else see the bob in her head? The loosey-goosey way her neck jiggles? Before everyone came, I was here alone with her and her fingers froze up in a weird position out of the blue. She pretended not to be scared, but she kept repeating that her mother had had a stroke right before she died. One side of my mother's body is significantly higher than the other and she is starting to look scrunched up like a character out of a fairy tale. She can't move her right shoulder and she takes Vioxx every day so that it doesn't hurt more than she can stand. And she's completely antisocial. She doesn't want to talk to anyone. She just wants to ration towels and reminisce about when her house was tidy.

I don't know how many more of these summers there will be. My mother moves faster and faster as if she can outrun the natural progression of getting older. She takes more trips, makes more plans, works out harder with her trainer. She is convinced that slowing down, like a "person of her age" should, will be the end of her. Not only will it kill her, but it will guarantee that her death will be a slow and incremental and agonizing one. Whereas if, on the other hand, she keeps moving, she will simply drop dead one day—quick and painless and maybe before they ask her to retire. I pointed out the unscientific nature of her thinking, in a foolhardy attempt to get her not to make dinner tonight.

"That's right. I just want to drop dead one day," she answered.

"But you can't control how you die, Mom, only how you live. I wish you would slow down and enjoy things a little more. Please don't run around all day shopping for groceries. Why don't you just enjoy that we're all here. We'll eat what's in the fridge or drive out for clams."

"I am enjoying my life, thank you very much," she told me. "And please close the door on your way out."

She can't stop long enough to notice all the lovely ways her grandchildren are interacting. The games they have invented with her hammock, the peals of laughter that flutter through the open summer windows like butterflies. She is on vacation. She has time on her hands but she is not an introspective person. Immersing herself in her family history—a history that she authored—is not an activity she has allotted time for. Dropping dead and making dinner are. So she is in the kitchen banging pots and slamming drawers. No one wants dinner. We'd rather have her enjoy our company. But one by one everyone enters and exits the kitchen, as my mother makes it abundantly clear that she does not want any help. At five o'clock she discovers she can't lift her right arm anymore. After shucking all the corn she can't reach up to get the pot to cook it in. She is humble and human for about ten minutes. At five-ten she is back to her old self and tells us, "I do not need to be watched. Out. Everyone out until dinner is ready."

At nine o'clock I go up to her room where the television is blaring. I curl up on her bed. She puts her arm around me. The skin on her arm is dry and wrinkled and flabby and hangs off her. She looks like my grandmother, who was an old lady to me the entire twenty years I knew her. By the time she was eighty she couldn't drive, she had trouble getting around her house, and they moved her to a little apartment. People had to come and give her groceries and nurses came to check up on her and administer her twenty medications three times a day.

My mother still drives, with total confidence. She still runs her department. She still goes to the gym. She goes to Venice and Ireland and San Francisco four times a year for work. She goes to the country every weekend. But she's fading. I am too. My eyelashes and eyebrows are so pale I feel like I have to draw arrows on my face with eyeliner and mascara to indicate I have eyes. It is like the lightening of hair is every body's way of preparing for its final and complete disappearing act: death. My mother is thirty-six years ahead of me in the process of aging. I am not ready for her to disappear. My mother has told me my whole life to do everything with grace and integrity. I try. But when she dies I will not be graceful. I will not be full of integrity. I will be clumsy and self-indulgent and depressed and unable to hold on. I can't even think about it.

"My skin is awful. It looks just like my mother's," she says.

"No it doesn't." It is the first lie I have ever told her. "How is your shoulder?"

"It hurts."

"Maybe you should do your physical therapy."

"I don't like to. It hurts. The Vioxx works."

"But the Vioxx isn't making it better."

"It does make it better. It reduces the inflammation."

"I know, but it's not solving the real problem. The real problem has to be solved by making the muscles around it stronger and loosening the joints and making the whole thing more flexible."

"I'll wait till I go back to the gym. I don't remember how to do the exercises the physiotherapist gave me."

"Do you have the sheet? I'll help you. You've got to do your exercises. That's how you're going to get better." She doesn't say anything. "Mom. I'll help you," I say again.

"I don't want you to help me," she tells me and turns up the volume on her television set.

GRACE AND INTEGRITY

I am at the doctor's office waiting for a Pap smear and having an epiphany. The woman next to me is holding a newborn. He is resting in her arms, reconciling his current routine against the memory of the warm fluid that used to be his life. He gazes at his mother with big wide eyes that can only see a few inches in front of him. She is his compass; without her he's lost. I know it like the back of my hand. I remember when Olive was born. We lay there in a slippery heap, like survivors from a Grimm's fairy-tale journey through the dark woods of childbirth, exhausted and euphoric. In my stupor, I realized that they were cutting the cord. We were becoming separate people for the first time since conception. Then they put her on my breast and she started nursing and we were reconnected. I was her life force again. She grew before my eyes from my milk. Taking care of an infant is so intimate. There is no hour of the day or night that is too early or late. There is no body fluid that is disgusting; there is no need that is inappropriate to fill. There is nothing that is off-limits.

My mother knew me when I was that helpless, when my life and death was as simple as getting enough milk. Late one summer afternoon when I was nine or ten my mother was rubbing my back. She rubbed under my shirt in circles like she'd done my whole life and as her hand moved toward my behind I felt horror and embarrassment where there once was none. She was taking liberties that were no longer hers. Sure, when I was a baby and my behind was still a tushie and not on its way to becoming my ass, she could touch it and wipe it and squeeze it and tickle it, but not *now*. But how can a mother be respectful of boundaries when there used to be none? When she changed diapers, did around-the-clock feedings, and was allowed and encouraged to kiss and tickle every square inch of her perfect little baby's body anytime?

Yesterday, getting Olive dressed, she said, "Kiss me, Mama," and I kissed her all over her satiny skin until she squealed like a little pig. I can't imagine ever not wanting to do that. Will that desire stop when she is in college? When she has her own apartment? Will I mind my own business when she has friends that I don't think are nice enough to her? Decisions to make that I fear she is avoiding? The umbilical cord is cut. Eventually—inevitably—a velvet rope replaces it. The mother, who always had the best seat in the house, has to wait on line outside in the cold. Two weeks ago Olive was feverish and clammy and throwing up. She lay in my arms moaning over and over, "I want my mommy. I want my mommy." I was right there, holding her, but that's all she could manage to say. It's so primal. And when I don't want to crawl back inside my mother I want her to leave me the fuck alone.

On my left in the doctor's office is the whole story in reverse. Two people so far ahead in time they are practically at the beginning. An old woman is gently trying to prod a glove onto the hand of what I realize is a very very old man. He is in a wheelchair wrapped in a blanket like a little baby tucked into its stroller. He drifts in and out of consciousness, back and forth between his inevitable future and what remains of this life. He can't even hold his head up. I'm sure she dresses him, feeds him, bathes him, soothes him, comforts him, sings to him, undresses him, does a million other tender personal things that would be too demeaning or inappropriate with a person able to take care of himself. They are bound by the intimacy of dependence. She smiles at him and it's obvious she is his everything.

I don't want to end up there. I want to stay young forever. I want my mother to be my mother forever. I want Olive to be my baby forever. This morning before I left for my appointment she asked, "Mommy, will you always take care of me?" And I said—way happier than I'm sure is appropriate—"Yes, I will. I will always take care of you. As long as you want me to." My husband said, "Mama will always look after you until you have to take care of her." One day I will be old. I will need help. Everything I take for granted will be difficult, maybe impossible. I could be like my friend's mother who became incontinent. I could be like my mother whose head bobs like Katharine Hepburn's even though I pretend it doesn't. I hope I have the grace of this old woman taking care of this old man. I hope I will have the tenderness and the patience and the class. But I doubt I will. I didn't show it this summer when my mother was falling apart. I was crass and callow. We both were. Neither of us was comfortable with the idea of what lay ahead. But I was not only grateful but happy to do it for Olive when she came to me. I better be able to do it when my mother is leaving me.

My mother calls. "I have to go out with Phillip tonight," she says.

"That's nice," I say, because I happen to be entertaining a fantasy that she will marry Phillip. And we will be rich. Very rich. And I will finally have, as an adult, what I have longed for as a child: parents.

"No it's not. He's an enormous bore. He's taking me to the opera."

"I love the opera."

"Well you should be going with him then. He is so boring I could die. He's sending a car to pick me up. Last year he took me to the Four Seasons, for my birthday. Isn't that awful?"

"It sounds pretty nice to me. He's so nice to you."

"Well I'm not impressed. The man has no center. He is like a bunch of qualities with absolutely nothing holding him together." And she hangs up.

My aunt Phyllis called me three times today. Everyone says she is losing her short-term memory. There was a time, in college, when I was sort of close to my aunt Phyllis. She knew I wasn't getting along with my mother and she tried to carve a niche in my misery. I let her. My aunt always kept the drapes closed, the furniture covered in plastic, and cooked all her food for at least four hours in a four-hundred-degree oven with onion soup mix or cream of mushroom soup or cornflakes or all three on top. She kept all her fancy clothes in the basement in a chicken-wire closet. After one trip to Ottawa she sent me home with three perfect Kate Pierson B-52s vintage party dresses. I was the envy of the Barnard club scene that year.

"Your sister called me today," I tell my mother.

"Ugh."

"She's coming on Monday," I say.

"I know. She called me four times today. What is she bothering you for? She must have gotten confused and thought you were me. She doesn't remember anything."

"She wanted me to beg you to see her," I say.

"I told her I would see her for Christ's sake," my mother says. "She is so impossible, I can't help it if the only time she has free I'm teaching. I told her to take an earlier plane. But she wouldn't. I told her there were planes leaving every hour and to just come in earlier. But of course she can't do that. Now instead of a husband making her life unlivable she's got this Karen making her life impossible."

The next day my cell phone rings. "Cathy, it's Phyllis," my aunt says. Her voice sounds unsure. It is unusual for her to call two days in a row. I usually speak to her once every few years and she only calls when I am about to do something like merge into speeding traffic at rush hour. Today I happen to be at a callback for a commercial.

"Yes, Aunt Phyllis," I say. I sort of can't stand my aunt Phyllis, and I sort of like her. If my mother had any relationship with her whatsoever I would too.

"I'm coming to New York on Monday," she says.

"I know," I say like we didn't go through this five times yesterday. "I'm looking forward to seeing you."

"Will I see your mother?" she asks. I can hear her panic mounting.

"I don't know. Did you make a plan?"

"She said she wouldn't see me." She sounds near tears.

"I thought she said she was teaching and she tried to find another time to see you," I say in an idiotic attempt to help them both.

"Is that what she said?" my aunt says. "Well I wish she would talk to me. She wouldn't take my calls." I hear her fumbling with a Kleenex.

"I would like to see you. When can I see you?"

"I don't know. I'm with my friend Karen."

"Could I see both of you?" I offer.

"Oh I don't know. I'm with my friend, it's very complicated."

"What time do you get in?" I ask.

"I don't know. Karen made all the arrangements."

"Well maybe you could call her and find out so we can make a plan," I suggest.

"Oh I don't know. But please ask your mother to call me."

"I will." And my aunt hangs up.

Three minutes later the phone rings again.

"Cathy? It's Auntie Phyllis."

"Hi, Aunt Phyllis."

"I'm coming to New York," she says.

"I know."

"I'm seeing a doctor. I'm not well."

"I'm sorry to hear that. Do you think I could see you?" I ask as though it will be easier to make a plan this time.

"Oh I would love to," my aunt says. She sounds like the saddest person in the world. "It will be my last time in New York. I'm seeing a doctor."

"I know. Well, when can I see you?" I ask feebly.

"I don't know. I'm with my friend Karen."

"Where are you staying? Maybe I could come up to your hotel?"

"I don't know where I'm staying. Don't you see? Karen made all the arrangements. Have you spoken to your mother?"

"Not yet."

"Please, beg her to see me," my aunt pleads.

"I will," I say. And I can't believe that I am still trying to repair their broken-down relationship. They haven't gotten along for more than half a century. Who am I kidding? "But regardless of what happens between you two I'd like to see you."

"I'd like to see you too. But I just don't know. I'm with my friend Karen."

"I'd be happy to see both of you. Why don't you talk to her and then let me know."

"Okay, dear," she says to me, like I am a four-year-old who just came up with an overly simplified solution to the war in the Middle East that will never work. Five minutes later she calls again.

"Cathy? It's Phyllis."

"Hi, Phyllis."

"I'm coming to New York on Monday," she tells me.

"Yes I know," I say. "I hope I can see you."

"I don't think I'll be able to. I'm coming with my friend Karen and I don't think she'll let me."

"What do you mean she won't let you?" I say. I sound exactly like my mother.

"It's very complicated, but I'm coming with my friend Karen and she is arranging everything and I can't just do whatever I please."

"Surely she won't mind if I come to your hotel and see you for twenty minutes for a cup of coffee in the lobby." This Karen person sounds awful.

"I don't know," my aunt says.

"Well I don't see how that could be a problem," I say losing my patience.

"I can't just come into the city you know," she says in a full-blown panic.

"I know. I'll come in, you don't have to go anywhere. I'll come to you."

"I don't know, I would love to see you. But I'm with Karen and she doesn't want to see you."

"She doesn't even know me."

"I know, but it's very complicated. I'm not alone, I'm with my friend Karen don't you see."

"Your friend doesn't sound like a very good friend if she won't let you see your niece."

"Well she said I could see you, but really I can't, you see."

"No. I don't. But whatever." I hang up and turn my attention back to my audition. I read over my copy, fill out my size card, and wait to be assigned a make-believe husband.

"Mom, your sister called me again today," I tell her when I get home.

"Ugh, what is she doing? She has no short-term memory you know. She's driving me crazy. Why is she calling you? You don't speak to her do you? When was the last time you spoke to her?"

"Yesterday, but before that probably three years."

"She's coming with her friend Karen. They're going to see some doctor about her memory. I'm meeting them there."

"You are? She said you wouldn't see her."

"She always says that. She tells you one thing and me something else. She's been that way her whole life. It makes me nuts. Of course I'm meeting her at the doctor's. It's the only time I can see her. I don't want to. I'm dreading the whole thing. I hung up last night after the fifth call and I was half crazy."

"Do you want me to come too?"

"Don't be ridiculous. I can manage."

"I know you can manage, but since you're dreading it, maybe it would make it easier if you had someone there with you."

"Well it's absolutely unnecessary."

"I know. But I would like to. I'm not doing anything Monday and I don't want you to have to go alone."

"I won't be alone. That Karen person will be there."

"I know you won't *literally* be alone. You are so annoying. But if it would make it easier for you I would like to go. Plus it will probably be the only time I can see her."

"What do you want to see her for? I wish I didn't have to see her."

The next morning my mother forwards me an e-mail from my aunt's friend Karen explaining how Phyllis desperately doesn't want to see me.

"Did you get the e-mail?" she asks on the phone.

"Yes. It sort of upset me."

"Shit. Why? I sent it to you so you wouldn't be upset. And so that you would see that she's crazy."

"Well I wasn't upset until I found out that she didn't want to see me. Why did you send it to me?"

"Oh for Christ's sake, so you could see what I am dealing with. She doesn't even know what she's saying. She's always pitting Peter against Paul and tries to play both sides down the middle. She's manipulative, and that is how she controls things. The one interesting thing her friend Karen said was that last year she took Phyllis to see a shrink and the shrink said Phyllis's memory is so bad that she panics because she can't keep her stories straight and she's afraid of being found out. I'm sure she *does* want to see you, she just doesn't remember; she doesn't remember anything. She has no memory and she just panics. But please. You shouldn't feel bad. It's me she's mad at. She doesn't know what she's saying. Don't you remember what happened with my mother's mink coat?"

"No."

"Your sister wanted it. It was the only thing of Bubbe's that she wanted after she died, and my sister took it. She had it cut up and turned into a jacket. And I said, 'Phyllis, that is the meanest thing you have ever done. You knew that Leslie wanted that coat and you deliberately took it and I will never forgive you.' And so she had it put back together and sent it to Leslie and Leslie said she didn't want it because it didn't smell like Bubbe anymore and that was the only reason she'd wanted it in the first place."

"Well I guess I won't see you at the doctor's."

"I guess not. You're not going to miss anything."

That night I get a weepy message from my aunt. "Cathy, dear, if I was rude, if I said something I shouldn't have, I sincerely apologize. I am truly sorry. I am not well and I am not responsible, but I am sorry if I said or did anything to make you feel bad."

I call her the next morning hoping I can catch her before her flight to New York and tell her I want to see her at the doctor's.

"Phyllis?"

"Cathy? I'm so sorry."

"Please. Don't worry about it. Really it's fine. I'll see you at the doctor's."

"The doctor's? You can't come to the doctor's."

"Why not? It's the only way I can see you."

"Well I don't know, it will be wonderful to see you I suppose. But I don't know you're coming."

"What do you mean? I just told you."

"I know. But I don't know. I'm going to act as though I am surprised. Because I don't know you're coming and it will be a surprise."

"But everyone knows I'm coming."

"But don't tell your mother you're coming."

"She already knows."

"But then how will I *act surprised*?" she says in a panic.

"I don't know. You seem to be the only one who wants to be surprised. Everyone else knows."

"Your mother's coming to the doctor's?"

"Yes. Karen and my mother and I are all coming."

"Well I don't know that you're coming. And I am going to be surprised. What a wonderful surprise."

"Okay. I'll see you later."

"But I don't know you're coming."

"Right," I say. I hang up and immediately call my mother.

"What do you mean you're coming to the doctor?" she yells at me. "You can't come. It's too many people!"

"Mom, we talked about it yesterday and I already told Phyllis I was coming."

"You didn't tell her I was coming did you?"

"Of course I did."

"But she didn't know I was coming!"

I hang up shaking. I meet them at the memory doctor at two o' clock. The waiting room is full of people in various states of psychic and physical disrepair. Old women with daughters, couples, one old man alone who can't remember what chair he was sitting in. He holds on to the nurse like she's a present sent from an escort service. I can tell my mother is freaked out. She is staring at everyone praying to God she doesn't resemble anyone here now, or ever. I'm sure she's trying to remember where she put the Hemlock Society recipe. My aunt looks amazing. I always think of her as what my mother ran away from, the life she escaped. The person she painstakingly defined herself against. Provincial and small-minded. But when my aunt walks into the waiting room she looks anything but provincial. She looks fantastic, in her smart gray suit and brand-new black Ferragamo pumps. In fact she looks a lot more energetic than the matronly well-dressed middle-aged pear-shaped woman she walks in with who must be Karen. My aunt hasn't aged since she was fifty. She looked terrifying then with her tiny up-turned-nose-job-nose and her freshly stretched face-lifted skin. Even her makeup and false nails and her lacquered hair were scary, but she looks great now.

"Oh, Cathy, it's wonderful to see you. How old are you?" she asks both hands on my shoulders, smiling deeply at me.

"Well," I say, smiling back, "I'm only going to tell you because you're going to forget. I'm forty-three."

"Forty-three?" My mother says, "You are not forty-three. You are forty-two."

"No. I just had a birthday. I'm forty-three."

"Forty-three? What year is this?" my mother asks. "This is not 2004."

"Yes it is, Mom."

"Holy shit," my mother says. They call my aunt in. The memory doctor is about twenty-seven years old. I could almost be his mother. This makes me nervous, but then I feel a little better because by the time I need him he'll be old enough to seem like he knows something. Doctor Junior tells us to sit down.

"Well, before I examine Phyllis," he says, "I just wanted to meet everyone and get their impressions of how things are going. Phyllis? How are things going?"

"Fine. But what do I know? I don't remember anything," my aunt says.

"How's your sleep?"

"Fine. I think," she looks at Karen for corroboration. Karen nods.

"Appetite?"

"Fine."

"She has no appetite. She eats like a bird. She's never eaten," my mother interjects. The doctor looks back at my aunt.

"But it's the same. It hasn't changed," my aunt says defending herself.

"Okay. As long as it hasn't changed. What kinds of problems are any of you noticing?"

"She's more panicked," my mother says. "She calls me ten times in a row sometimes. And doesn't remember."

"Really. How often do you speak to your sister?" the doctor asks Phyllis.

"Never," Phyllis says.

"I call her every week to ten days," my mother says to the doctor but not to Phyllis.

"That's not true," my aunt says to the doctor, but not to my mother.

"Yes, it is, Phyllis," my mother says.

"Well I don't remember. And usually when I forget something and someone reminds me it jogs my memory. But I do not remember my sister calling me."

"It's true that in the past you could retrieve your memories," the doctor says, "so during the examination we'll see where that's at, but it is possible that sections are disappearing and you don't have access to them anymore."

"No," my aunt says as though that is the living end. Karen nods yes.

"There are things you don't remember anymore Phyllis," Karen tells my aunt.

"How often do you speak to Phyllis?" the doctor asks Karen.

"About six times a day. And I have noticed a change."

"Okay, well why don't you all step out and I will examine Phyllis and then I'll have you come back in."

"Only Karen should come back in. She is the one that is really connected," my mother says. She has now relinquished responsibility to Karen.

"Okay. Only Karen," says the nice young doctor. We all exit so he can examine Phyllis.

"It's so difficult with Phyllis," Karen says to us.

"It's impossible with Phyllis," my mother says to Karen. We stand next to each other like precariously placed objects on high shelves in an earthquake zone. When the doctor pokes his head out, he gestures only for Karen. My mother and I find our way back to the waiting room. A few minutes later Karen and Phyllis emerge. Karen sits down next to my mother while Phyllis goes to the front desk to schedule another appointment. Even fifteen feet away the resemblance between my mother and her facially reconstructed sister is remarkable. They have the same mannerisms, the same body language, and they share the same impatience with people they think are too slow. My aunt is so clearly annoyed with the office personnel and from this angle she could be my mother. Or me, for that matter.

"Well, it's Alzheimer's. Full blown," Karen reports to us while Phyllis is still out of earshot.

"Oh my God," I say.

"The doctor said she shouldn't live alone anymore because in six months to a year she will be in danger of setting herself on fire or wandering outside in her nightgown and freezing to death. But she won't live in a home. She's very stubborn. He tried to get her to see that she should do it now while the choice is still hers. But she's very stubborn. I don't know what I'm going to do because it is getting to be more than I can handle. I'm going to have to turn it over to her children. I just have to. I have no choice. It's just too much for me."

"She is too much for everyone. She's impossible. She's pushed everyone away her whole life," my mother says.

On the way out of the office I wrestle with my aunt for the handle of her suitcase. But she is very determined to carry it herself. "I'm going to kill myself," she says quietly to no one. "I am just going to kill myself." My poor aunt hoists her bag into the cab herself and we all say goodbye.

Walking to the subway I ask my mother, "Were you freaked out by all the people in the waiting room?"

"God yes," she says.

"I thought you were. You're not like that," I tell her. "You're not," I say again. "Are you afraid of getting Alzheimer's?"

"Of course I am."

"How do you think your memory is? Because I happen to know a very nice doctor."

"Not great. I know I forget things. But I think it's normal."

"Okay," I say.

"I can't stand to see my sister. It makes me crazy. I see so much of myself in her and I can't stand it."

"Like what?"

"Just physical things." After a while she says, "Do you know that today was the first day I left the gym before my session was over? I finished my treadmill and then I just got up and went home. I was too tired. I couldn't do any more."

"I'm sure it had something to do with your sister and seeing her today."

"God I hope so."

At the six train we say goodbye.

"Mom, if you want to call me later, I'm here."

"*I'm* not the one with Alzheimer's, you know."

"I know," I say. I don't allow myself to react to the snarl in her voice. "I don't think you are. I just think you are a person with a lot on your mind and I am a person who loves you. If you need me, please use me."

She stares blankly into my face, then grips the handrail and descends the stairs.

"Guess what?" my mother says breathlessly. "Someone just gave me their tickets to *King Lear* tonight with Christopher Plummer. They are house seats. They are fabulous seats. Would you like to go? I thought you would like to go. Let's go. Would you like to go?"

The fountain at Lincoln Center is dotted with people relishing the warm night, and the white buildings with their confident architecture, juxtaposed against the trees in bloom, are so stunning I want to stop and linger, but I can't because I'm late. In a cruel twist of fate my mother, after making me be a person who is chronically late, changed her ways and is now always early. Standing just inside the front door she looks small. She has been waiting for me. I want to yell into the flurry of people descending into the theater around her, "Hey, watch out for my mother. Excuse me, my mother is there, please, be careful!" My mother the maverick, the one who cuts me to the quick and cures me with equal grace, the person who taught me everything I value and hate, my genetic other half, looks like something left outside in a snowstorm. I want to bring her inside. To dry her off, to warm her up, to bundle her up. Her age has arrived. I've been giving it the slip. Running ahead of it, not listening when it clearly called me, but it just slapped me on the back. I've been served. Witnessing it like this, in public, is so much more upsetting than I can believe.

"These lines are impossible," my mother says, scanning the room, snapping me back into reality. "Go stand on that one, maybe you'll get through first and we can sit down." Whatever thoughts I was grappling with disintegrate as I focus on the task at hand—hurrying up. My mother doesn't live in this moment. She craves the next moment, the one coming up. If Olive were old enough to wait on lines by herself I would send her off too. It occurs to me at the supermarket to send Olive off to another line. I get excited about how much faster everything will go and then I look down and see how little she is. She is too young to go wait on a line by herself, so I stay put. I seriously pray that by the time she is big enough to wait on another line I will have realized how much nicer waiting with someone is. Even if it takes four minutes longer, even if it takes forty minutes longer, companionship trumps speed. I never knew that until I knew Olive. I don't think my mother ever knew that.

"Red? Is that you?" a man calls out from a third line.

"Oh my lord," my mother says, turning around. There is significantly less enthusiasm in her voice than the voice that addressed her. "Lionel."

"It's been what? Thirty years," he says.

"Must be," my mother says. She grabs hold of her hands to stop them from shaking. Her hands have a life of their own that she is not proud of. I have never thought of her as vulnerable to what other people think.

"Are you still in Rye?" my mother asks.

"Yes, we are."

"With the second wife? The one you found in Paris?"

"I'm sorry?"

"With your second wife," my mother says. It's not always clear if my mother doesn't like the person she is speaking to or if she thinks that common courtesy is something special reserved for geniuses and other extraordinary people in the world. Growing up she always told me "Ordinary is not acceptable."

"Yes. And you?" Mr. Ordinary asks.

"Still in the city. How are the kids?"

"Wonderful, one's an A&R man and the other one is running a dot-com. How are yours?"

"Great. Here is one of them," she says pointing to me ten feet away in my line. "Cathy, do you remember going to Lionel's house in Rye?"

"Mmhmm," I lie, with big a friendly smile on my face. I want to bestow common courtesy on the common man. But I am my mother's daughter and a big smile on my face is probably imperceptible to the naked eye. To the naked eye I am probably just garden variety rude.

"What are you up to?" my mother asks. She seems a little surprised that she's still talking to him.

"Retired and loving it," he says. "You?"

"Not retired and loving it," my mother says a little too quickly.

"Wonderful, good for you," the retired ordinary gentleman from Rye says and bids us adieu.

My mother and I and her disobedient hands go to our seats.

"Aren't these fabulous seats? They're house seats. They're fabulous, my friend gave them to me," she says. "Do you know any of these actors?"

"Actually no," I say looking at the Playbill. "It looks like they're all from Stratford."

"I have to go to the bathroom. I'll be right back," my mother announces. "I'll come too," I say. "It's a long show."

There is only one line for the bathroom so we wait together. My mother glances at her Playbill again and asks me, "Do you know any of these actors?"

"No, Mom. I don't. It looks like they're mostly from Stratford."

"*Stratford*? Ontario?" she says as though that were shocking information. Did she forget we covered this or was she not listening?

"Yes. That's where this production originated." The last time I read *King Lear* I was a junior in high school. It blew me away. I remember thinking it was a story about arrogance and truth. Tonight it is all about aging. Christopher Plummer has thrown himself into the role of a man losing his grip. His mind and his children are all walking out on him. He stands on stage, a lonely shadow of a once ferocious king, trying to hang on to what he can make sense of, with two hands that flap like sheets in the wind. He is so desperate and lost and furious. I am sitting next to my mother and all I can think about is the dead skin, the dried brain cells, the lifeless eggs, the collagen, our wasted youth, and the vitality piling up in a heap on the floor by our feet. I don't have the rest of my life for everything anymore. Certain opportunities have passed. I am too old for them now. I won't have more children. I will never get to play Franny if they ever make the movie of *Franny and Zooey*. This is what getting old is: The end is visible and your plans and ambitions have to be adapted. Your options are no longer limitless. And on top of that, your body leaves you behind to fend for yourself. Aging is so much more awful than I was prepared for and I am dealing only with the beginning of it myself. And sitting next to my mother watching the aging king battle the elements and his mortality and his mind is almost more than I can handle.

"Let's go on a trip," I suggest a few weeks later. I am nostalgic for our youth.

"Sure," she says. "For our birthdays. Where would you like to go? Spain to see the new Gehry Museum? Should we go to Paris for a weekend? It's Javier's birthday in April, he just invited me to Brazil to celebrate. We could do that."

I hang up wondering why I don't have the energy my mother does. I e-mail her a link to a spa called Miraval Life in Balance.

"I don't care for it," she e-mails me back. "It's too spiritual. What about Mexico City?" "Can't handle the time difference. Too hard on the back end," I reply. I spend all my spare time looking for concepts for our trip—something that will relax me and be exciting enough for her. It is exhausting. A week later she calls. "I found the place. It's nine thousand dollars for the week and we each get a facial or a massage every day and I am booking it," she announces. She forwards me the link to the Miraval Web site. I don't tell her that it's the same place I sent her a link for three weeks ago. Actually I try but she doesn't believe me.

I have never been away from Olive for this long. I fill a box with eight stones and tell Adam that she can take one out every day as a way of measuring the time till I come home. I write her a book of letters she can read and draw in while I'm gone. I am suddenly five years old, thirty-three pounds, living on Park Avenue, anguished until my parents return from Europe or the Far East or wherever they are. All I want is the day before they come back to get here so I can make their WELCOME HOME sign. In bed that night I imagined them, next to each other on the plane, saying, "I wonder what kind of sign she made this time? I can't wait to see it, can you?" Maybe the signs meant as little to them as the dolls they brought me.

I kill myself to arrive at my mother's building at 7:30 a.m., the designated time. I am prompt, but she is already waiting for me downstairs and her luggage is already in the car she ordered to take us to the airport.

"I had the hardest time packing," she says, landing clumsily on the seat next to me. "I am a terrible packer. I was freezing the whole time at the Golden Door. I was miserable. I brought too many things and they were all the wrong things."

"Oh my God, do you remember that summer in Aspen when you packed my snowpants?" I say, looking out at the inside of the Holland Tunnel.

"No I do not. I didn't bring snowpants. Did I?"

"You did. You said, 'You never know and it is better to have them and not need them than to need them and not have them.' And I am just realizing that I am such a sucky packer because your voice saying 'better to have it and not need it than to need it and not have it' is my mantra and I pack everything."

"Did it snow?" she asks.

"It did. And I was furious." On the other side of the Holland Tunnel we notice we are wearing the same brand of hiking shoes.

"How much?" she asks.

"Ninety-four dollars."

"Mine were eighty," she says sadly. "I like yours better."

At the curb she won't let us check our bags. "I don't check," she tells the skycap irritably. The e-ticket machine is not working, so we schlep our luggage, which we are not checking, to the ticket counter. My mother presents an itinerary printed in an oversized font and enclosed in clear plastic, like a book report, to a languid Mexican woman who can find no record of our reservation. "Well no wonder I couldn't get the machine to work," my mother says to me. "I don't understand," she says to the Delta agent. "They took the miles out of my account. Here is the confirmation number." She pushes her printed itinerary across the counter for the woman to have a closer look.

"You never booked this," the agent says flatly.

"What are you talking about? What do you mean?" And then to me she says, "This is not happening."

"This is a hold for a ticket, but you were supposed to confirm it and you didn't and now there are no seats left." The lady slides the itinerary back across the counter and sure enough, on the bottom in little letters it says, "not a reservation; subject to change or cancellation." All the color drains from my mother's face as she says, "I have been traveling for years and this has never happened. Nothing like this has ever happened. This is ridiculous. I don't know what to say. Do you have room on another flight?"

"No," the agent says.

"What about standby, what about tomorrow? What about returning on a different day? Do you have a supervisor? Do you have an imagination? Is there a customer service person? This is ridiculous." The woman picks up the phone and calls customer service. I gesture her over while she is on hold with the supervisor. I tell her conspiratorially, "We planned this trip a long time ago. I made arrangements for child care for my daughter . . . Isn't there anything you can do? I don't know if we will be able to go another time, *if you know what I mean*." We both look over at my delicate mother huddled over her itinerary. The agent tells me she is trying and hands the phone to my mother who starts yelling, "Yes yes yes I know. I heard you the first time! Stop repeating yourself. I am not interested in the same information over and over again. I am interested in some assistance." Then to us she says, "I cannot stand this woman. You know these people who simply recite information by rote and have no intake—" I take the phone away from her.

"Hello," I say smiling into the receiver like an ambassador's wife at a UN cocktail party.

"Yes, as I said, you did not book the ticket and there is nothing I can do," the disembodied voice of customer service says.

"Hi. I am actually her daughter. How are you?"

"Your mother did not book her ticket correctly and there is no availability for mileage-plus seats at this time."

"I understand," I say. "Is there any way we could go standby or try to pay for tickets?"

"Your mother did not book her ticket correctly and there is no availability," she snaps at me.

"Listen," I snap back. "I am just a person, at an airport with my mother, trying to go on a long-awaited vacation. Please try to speak to me like a human being. Please don't yell at me." The ticket agent takes the phone from me and tries to talk to the supervisor. My mother hits me and says, "At least *this* one is trying. That one on the phone could give a shit. This one cares. A little, I think." And somehow, after fifteen minutes on the phone with the supervisor, and ten minutes of maneuvering letters and numbers and magic symbols on her keyboard, we end up on the same flights we were supposed to be on in the first place. But now we are late and have to run to our gate, with our unchecked bags. I am amazed at the elegance and agility with which my mother removes and replaces her shoes when we go through security. I, on the other hand, am having a heart attack. My mother is eyeing me and my whole childhood is replaying before me: "You're too slow. You are too slow. Move it." When we finally pass through security and get our clothes back on, we are stopped at our gate.

"Ma'am, you have too many bags," they tell my mother, gesturing to the large brown Prada duffle she has filled with *Vanity Fair*, *The New Yorker*, toiletries, and her medication. "You have to leave that brown suitcase here. You are only allowed one carry-on."

"This is my purse," my mother explains, holding up her purse.

"The other one. You have to check the other one." The Delta lady sees right through my mother's bait-and-switch attempt.

"My medication is in it. I need my medication," my mother says clinging to the bag.

"Take your medication out and check the bag. Hurry ma'am. The plane is boarding."

"I don't check bags. I never check bags," my mother says.

"Ma'am, this is the last time I am going to tell you. Sondra," she says to another navy-blue-suited Delta employee, "tell this woman she has too much stuff. Ma'am, you are holding up the flight."

"Mom, give me your bag," I command and take the bag from her. She looks on, helpless, as I rearrange all her carefully packed items willy-nilly inside my tote bag and shove her Prada bag back into her suitcase.

"Now *your* bag is too big," the lady says to me totally annoyed. "Oh, Sondra, I can't deal with this, it's your call." Sondra doesn't give a shit. They let us board.

Even though we are in first class we are only entitled to a half-ounce box of Special K, canned orange and grapefruit sections, a wrinkled white bun, and some plastic utensils for the three-and-a-half-hour, movieless flight to Atlanta. There is milk, it turns out, but you have to ask for it. When I ask for a pillow, the flight attendant explains, as though I should know better, "Those are quite an expense for us to maintain and customers complained about overhead storage anyway." After devouring my cereal I look behind to see what they are eating in coach, imagining it must be better. It is. Everyone brought their own food. Coach is rows of heads inhaling goodies from around the globe—burritos, pizza, hamburgers—I am flying with a bunch of refugees. Flying has become the most miserable pastime America has to offer.

My mother says disgustedly, "I remember when I used to get dressed up to fly."

In Tucson we call the spa to arrange our pickup. They must have told my mother to wait in baggage claim because I hear her yelling into her phone, "We didn't *check* anything. We are carrying our bags. We only have carry-on." She hangs up agitated, because even though we didn't check our bags, all the other spa arrivees did and we have to wait with them at the baggage carousel. Everyone else looks fresh and put together, in their matching velour workout suits.

A Miraval representative in his seventies welcomes us and shows us to the Miraval Life in Balance bus. Relaxing spa music is immediately siphoned through many invisible speakers like a noxious gas. "They don't do this at the Golden Door," my mother says to me. And then completely changing the subject, "Are there a lot of retired-person communities here?" she asks the driver.

"Oh sure," he says. "We have lots of communities up here. Most of us are from the one just a mile down from the spa. Beats just hanging around," he says, hoisting our bags out of the back of the van with an impressive amount of vigor.

My mother and I take in our new home. "The Golden Door is very Asian in feel. I don't know what to make of this," she says looking at the huge fireplace, the Indian rugs, the vaguely Santa Fe–style decor. We are given complimentary water bottles and tote bags by another retiree whose hair is the color of pale pink cupcake frosting. I wish Olive were here to see it. Another retiree named Roy takes us on a tour of the facility so we won't get lost while we are there. He shows us our room, the yoga building, the dining rooms, the swimming pools, the spa, the place where you sign up for hiking and horseback riding and cooking classes. He is just as nice as all the other retirees we have met. "The Golden Door is very different," my mother whispers. "It is very minimal. Very Japanese."

Over lunch she reminisces about her brother. "You know, I remember seeing *Schindler's List* with you and Barb when it came out and I went home and cried for a week. And I thought, *What the hell is wrong with me?* And I realized I was mourning my brother's death. We were never allowed to mourn him because my mother said he was coming back. She said he was missing and he would come back. We were never even allowed to say he was dead." After lunch we unpack and go to the spa building for our four o'clock massages. At dinner she is utterly perplexed as to why the girl who seated us is unable to bring us our dinner.

"She is the hostess," I explain.

"Yes. I still don't understand why she can't take our order. She works here. And why is that boy lurking and loitering about our table?" I explain that it is his job and that his manager probably doesn't want him lurking and loitering about in the kitchen because he was hired to take care of the customers. "Oh," she says. "You don't really have any idea what goes on in a restaurant, do you?" I say, realizing she has never had a service-oriented job. "You have always kind of been the boss, haven't you?" I say.

"What is it like to be a waiter?" she asks, not acknowledging the waitress who just put our food down.

"Horrible," I say, "because either you are treated like you aren't there, or people feel that they can talk to you about inappropriate things because you are just a waiter. And there is nothing you can do because it is your job to serve them." When we order dessert my mother actually looks our waitress in the face and smiles. I am touched.

Later in our room she says, "I wish I had known my father more."

"But I thought you loved him so much. You always talk about how gentle he was, how kind he was, how special he was."

"He was," she says. "But I never knew him. I never talked with him. I never knew what interested him, what he thought about. I never talked to him."

She lays out her hiking clothes in a neat pile for the next morning, which reminds me of the way we laid out my school clothes every night when I was little. I lie in my bed one nightstand away from my mother thinking this is the exact trip I wanted. Little things are being revealed effortlessly. I feel certain that by the end of the week we will have had a really special experience.

I am woken by the loudest snoring I have ever heard. I go to her bed alarmed. She looks like a ghost in the moonlight and I am scared to disturb her. I get back into bed. Eventually her snoring soothes me, and I panic when there is a moment of silence. In the morning she says, "Were you ever snoring last night! You woke me up! I couldn't get back to sleep, I had to take an Ambien!"

"Why didn't you wake me up?" I ask.

"I couldn't. You were sleeping so peacefully."

For breakfast I eat oatmeal, scrambled eggs, and bacon and have a pot of green tea. She has nothing.

"Shouldn't you eat something?" I say. "It's a two-hour hike. You should have something in your stomach."

"I liked it at the Golden Door. We hiked before breakfast. I don't like to eat before because I take this oil and everything comes right out of me and I need to go to the bathroom."

"Why don't you take your oil after the hike tomorrow instead?" I suggest.

"Oh. That's a good idea," she says. I momentarily feel like an adult.

The hike is gorgeous. The Sonora desert is like being in an animated Pixar film, art-directed by a genius. My mother agrees. "This is more beautiful than the Golden Door." There are three guides for our hike. One is a retiree named William. My mother hits me, "Again with the retirees." William helps her up a rocky hill and I hear her say, "I'm an old lady for Christ's sake." William says, grinning, all his good manners lined up in a row, "Well I never would have known." She loves him and she hates him.

Eventually my mother falls so far behind that William becomes her personal guide. It turns out he is an exceptionally strong hiker, even if he has spittle gathering at the corners of his mouth. Miles ahead I keep thinking about her, dependent and annoyed, at the mercy of the world's most boring nice man.

My mother spends the rest of the day coughing in the room. She seems to be allergic to something. She sleeps for the rest of the afternoon.

I go for a luxurious long swim in a beautiful pool tiled with stones. Then I take my camera and try to take pictures for Olive of all the bunnies that live on the property. There are also two amazing ducks I photograph. Then I meet my mother at the spa for our four o'clock massages. She looks half dead and is wearing her sunglasses; I guess it is her new thing. She seems unconcerned that she is wearing very dark glasses indoors. We sit in the relaxing room waiting for our therapists and she doesn't say a word. When her therapist comes to get her and says, "Hi, I'm Carla, how are you?" my mother just coughs in her face.

After the massages she says she feels shaky and awful. She doesn't eat anything at dinner and is coughing like crazy. "I am never going to sleep tonight because of this goddamn cough. Everyone is saying allergies are awful this time of year, but I never had any allergies in my life. I don't understand what is happening.

I am going to have to take an Ambien to knock myself out. I will never sleep with this cough," she says again.

"Why don't I get you some cough medicine or some lozenges?"

"Cough medicine doesn't do anything. I just want an Ambien."

"Okay. But I am sure some lozenges will make it easier on your throat."

"I just . . . want . . . to go to sleep," she says, a declaration wracked with hacking coughs. I call the front desk and ask for a humidifier and a ride to the drugstore. A lovely retiree takes care of both.

When I come back she is a nervous wreck. "What's the matter?" I ask.

"I just read the box of the allergy medicine you bought me this afternoon. It says you are not supposed to take it if you are taking certain medications."

"Why don't I call a pharmacist and ask. What is the name of your medicine?"

"I don't know. I didn't bring the bottle."

"Well why don't you call Freddy?"

"That's a good idea." And she calls her GP.

"What'd he say?"

"He said it's nothing, it just will make me a little jumpy. Give me my Ambien, will you?"

"I don't think you should take anything else, do you?"

"It's fine. It's a small dosage. It's the smallest dosage. I just really want to sleep or I will go crazy."

I get her a pill from the bathroom. She downs it and promptly says good night. She puts her head on her pillow, closes her eyes, and waits for sleep to arrive. I brush my teeth and wash my face and put out my clothes for the hike the next morning. I get into bed with Jonathan Safran Foer. I'm just getting comfortable when I hear my mother swatting her bed.

"Get the fuck off my bed," she says.

"Who is on your bed?" I ask, slightly alarmed.

"My mother's outside. She paid sixteen dollars for the car."

"Really?" I say. "Who else is here?"

"My whole family still lives on your street. Right on the corner. We got to get the blintzes and all that shit. Are you ready to go?"

"Where are we going?"

"To Peter's. I think I lost my script," she says. "I don't have my script. Who are my friends in the audience? Look, they're three deep. There's Jane Wyman. What do we have planned for my evening's entertainment?"

"Nothing," I say. "I think this is it. Mom? Are you asleep?"

"Of course not. Are you shipping all this to Ottawa?"

"Mom, it's time to go to sleep. Stop talking."

"Oh! Am I talking? I'm sorry."

It goes on like this for three more hours until she finally conks out. If I had not been told by my husband that I rave like a crazy person after taking an Ambien and having a little wine I would have been petrified. But I am sure it is just the Ambien, even though her ravings sound awfully close to senility.

The next morning she remembers nothing. I suggest she not take so much Ambien tonight because it seems to have quite an effect on her. She says, "That never happened before."

"How do you know?" I ask.

"I guess I don't. I don't usually have a roommate."

"Are you coming on the hike today?"

"No it's too much. It's too steep. That doctor got me hysterical about falling. That's all I need now is to break my hip."

"Why don't you arrange a private hike? And then it could be flatter."

"No."

"It's something they do here. It's one of the activities."

"No. I want to do the regular hike or I'm not going."

"Mom, let me call them. I'll even go too and then we can go slow and I can take pictures for Olive."

"That's enough, Cathy. Stop talking to me like I can't take care of myself. I don't want to go hiking."

She sits at breakfast wearing her sunglasses and an expression resembling a squashed pumpkin. I leave her alone in her misery and go hiking. She spends the rest of the day coughing and lying in the dark.

"Let's go home," I say at three o'clock. "You are obviously miserable. Wouldn't you rather be at home?"

"I am not miserable! I just have *terrible* allergies."

"Exactly, so let's leave and you won't have allergies anymore."

"No. I can stay. I want you to have a good time."

"I had a good time. Now let's go. Seriously it's not any fun knowing you are so uncomfortable. Let's go."

"I want you to enjoy yourself."

"I did, Mom. I really did." I change all the reservations while she lies on the bed in her sunglasses. I pack for both of us. I take special care folding all her things and I pack her bag like it is a picture, all the white things together, all the pink things together. I arrange all her clothes in descending color order.

At dinner I tell her, "I could sort of relate to what you said about mourning your brother, because I feel like I was so aware of how lucky I was to have had a good father for nine years and that it was bad to be manipulative, that I don't think I felt comfortable mourning Lloyd."

"You know what you did after he died? For about a year? Whenever something wasn't to your liking you would start to cry and say you missed your father."

"What?"

"You don't remember? For about a year. You don't remember? Isn't that something."

"No."

"Well that's what happened. Every time you were at a playdate and something wasn't to your liking, you would start to cry. I would get a call from the mother saying, 'Cathy's crying. She misses her father.' And I would have to pick you up. It happened all the time. It was your way of getting what you wanted."

"Maybe I did miss him."

"No. You didn't miss him. That is just what you did."

"How do you know?"

"Because the mother told me. She said everything was fine and then you just started crying. It is what you did. You look upset."

"I am upset. It is so ugly the way you assume a child is being manipulative."

"Cathy, this went on for a year. It wasn't just a couple of months. It was a year. You didn't still miss him. You look upset. Oh, I don't want you to be upset."

"I am. Why didn't you ever try and find out what I was upset about?"

"I didn't have to, the mother told me."

"But why didn't you talk to me?"

"I don't know," she says finally. "I don't want you to be upset. We have different notions. You can disagree but I don't want you to be upset."

"I am upset that we have such different ideas about how to treat people."

"But it's okay to be different"

"It is okay to be different, but who cares? I was upset about something and you didn't have any patience."

"I did, but not for that long."

"I know, and that is upsetting."

"How could I get you not to be upset?" she repeats, not because she understands what I am feeling but because it is awkward that I am feeling something.

"You could say you're sorry."

"All right," she says uncomfortably. "But what good would that do?"

"Because it would make me feel like you understood me. People like to feel *understood*." I hear myself trying to explain it to her. But it is like talking to another species.

"That didn't occur to me," my mother says. She looks like she is a hundred years old. She looks incapable of ever being my mother. "All right," she says. "Well I suppose I could have handled it differently." I think she means it but I can't see beyond her black lenses to know what she thinks.

"Thank you," I answer but feel nothing.

When I get back to Brooklyn I take an Ambien and finally crawl into bed at 2:00 a.m.

My husband rolls over and asks, "How is she? How was the rest of your trip?" I tell him about our last supper, how she said that all I did when things didn't go my way was say I missed my father. I tell him how I collected flowers for Olive so she could see how beautiful the desert was and how it amazed me that my parents used to travel for three weeks at a time and never give it a second thought—I was an infant left with some nurse in a starched white uniform whose bumpy bosom, and never her face, are in all the picture albums. That we lived in Great Neck for a while and the doctors thought the commute was too much on my father so my parents took an apartment in the city and commuted to their three children on Friday nights for the weekend. I tell him how I realized there was never anyone who took care of me and that no one helped me with my grief when my father died. I tell him how sad it was for me to watch my own mother unable to care for herself either—she was so angry at herself for getting sick, for being weak—and she couldn't nurture herself any better than she could nurture her children. I tell him how she left her copy of *The Magic Mountain* on the plane and a very sweet young man ran after us and returned it to her. I say I live for moments like that—moments of connection—and she doesn't even realize that these moments make up the fabric of our lives. She commented how nice it was of him to give her the book, but it was an isolated incident to her. Not the spinal cord of humanity. I hear myself say, with an ugliness that surprises both of us, "She's not human." My husband strokes my head and says, "Of course she is. There was just no way she could help you with your grief, don't you see? Because then she would have had to acknowledge her own."

"I had a friend named Sheila," Olive says to me in the kitchen.

"You did?" I wonder where she got that name. We don't even know anyone named Sheila.

"She died. I miss her very much."

"Oh. I'm sorry," I say.

"Mom?"

"Yes."

"Can I draw?"

"Yes. Will you use a piece of paper please instead of the table?"

"Okay."

"Here, honey." I give her some paper and markers and set her up at her table.

"You say no I can't draw and I will say yes I can draw."

"Okay. Ready?"

"Yes."

"Okay go."

"I can draw."

"No you can't."

"Yes I can."

"No you can't."

"Yes I can."

"No. I don't think you can."

"Yes I can."

"No. Really? You can?"

"Yes I can," she laughs. She shows me the person she drew. It's a big egg with a smile, two dots for eyes, and some hairs sticking straight up, growing out of the top like grass. Coming out of the bottom are two sticks with little branches at the ends, which are the person's legs and feet and toes. It has no neck and no body. It's the greatest person I ever saw.

"Do you like this person?" she asks.

"Yes I do. I really do."

"Her name is Lala and she had a sister named Sala but she died."

"Oh."

"She is very sad. She misses her very much."

"Sure, that's what happens."

"Do you miss your mom?"

"Actually I do today."

"But that's okay because she's not dead."

"That's true."

"But do you miss your dad?"

"Yes I do. I wish you could have met him."

"But that's okay because you have my daddy."

"Thank you, Olive."

"Mom?"

"Mmhmm?"

"Mom?"

"Yes."

"Mom?"

"Yes."

"Mom?"

"Yes my lovey."

"Mom?"

"Yes."

"Mommy? Why did your dad die?"

"Because . . . that's what happens. It's part of life. Everybody dies. You live your life and then you die."

"But why did he die?"

"I guess because he lived his life and it was time."

"Do you miss him?"

"Mmmhmm."

"Will I die?"

"One day."

"I don't want to."

"I know, honey. I don't think most people do. But, it's just part of what happens."

"Will you die?"

"Yup. One day. But hopefully not for a very long time."

"Because you will miss me too much?"

"Yes," I say, tracing a little constellation of freckles across her cheeks, "because I would miss you too much."

"Maybe that's why no one likes to die. Because then they can't say hi to everybody anymore. And it makes them miss them."

"I bet you're right," I tell her and squeeze her close. I swear I wish she could just crawl back inside me.

"You will be pleased to know I have pneumonia," my mother announces to me on the telephone.

"My god."

"I finally dragged myself to see Freddy yesterday. I thought I was dying. He couldn't believe I got out of bed and into a taxi. See I am not falling apart. I have goddamn pneumonia."

"Boy, I'm so sorry. Are you feeling better?"

"Not yet. I slept for fourteen hours last night. Maybe the antibiotics will kick in today. I knew it wasn't allergies. I just have pneumonia. That's why I couldn't do the hike. I can barely breathe. He said I have to stay home the rest of the week."

"Wow."

"And I have nodules."

"What?"

"I have nodules on my thyroid," she says.

"What does that mean?"

"I don't know, Cathy," she snaps. "I guess I have cancer."

"Wait a minute. What did Freddy really say?"

"Nothing. He made me an appointment with some endocrinologist tomorrow at nine."

"All right, well let's not jump the gun. You've had an overactive thyroid for forty years and you haven't gotten cancer yet."

"*I have nodules, Cathy,*" she repeats, and I can see that she has put herself on the conveyor belt at the crematorium already.

"I know you do. I'm just saying let's not jump the gun." But this is a ridiculous thing to say to a person who has made a lifestyle out of jumping the gun. It might even be a ridiculous thing to say to someone with an overactive thyroid. Maybe an overactive thyroid makes you jump the gun.

"I will tell you, Mom," I say, choosing my words very carefully. "I have two friends, both younger than me, who had thyroid cancer and they are both fine. It is very treatable. But I don't think you have cancer."

"I have *nodules*," she repeats like I am an imbecile.

My mother's endocrinologist, Dr. Holmes, is so handsome that I am sitting in the waiting room planning my next outfit in case we have a follow-up visit.

"I hate these specialists," my mother says just as I have settled on a navy blue vintage A-line skirt and Marc Jacobs shoes I got on sale three years ago. "They have exactly fifteen minutes allotted for each person because of the goddamn HMOs. Look how small this waiting room is. They've got us all crammed in here like a bunch of sardines." I can feel her terror like it was my own. Not only is she terrified of having cancer, she hates these specialists because she is not special to them. The doctor who she is special to is Freddy. But he can't help her with any of her latest ailments and this strikes me as yet another shitty thing about getting old. You work your whole life to cultivate a relationship with a doctor and then when you really need them, they send you to someone else.

"Well," Dr. Holmes says looking at her films when we are finally in his tiny, rather unimpressive office. "You have two nodules—"

"Yes," my mother says, interrupting him.

"—Two in the upper quadrant, one is cold, and the other one is hot," Dr. Holmes says, finishing his thought.

"Yes. My GP told me," my mother says gravely. I wish she'd take her sunglasses off.

"One of them is overproducing, which is fine, and the other one is underproducing. I am not at all concerned, but I think we should get them biopsied."

"Why?" my mother says, overwrought. I glance over to a shelf, filled with samples. I have got to figure out how to steal some Paxil for her. "If you are not concerned, why do I have to do something?" my mother pleads, holding onto her throat where the uninvited nodules lie.

"It is strictly procedure," Dr. Holmes says in a very reassuring voice. "When there is a cold nodule, it is a good idea to check it out, and while we're in there we should just check them both out, but I am honestly not at all concerned." He smiles gently. "I am scheduling you for biopsies. What is better for you, morning or afternoon?"

"I don't care," my mother says. "Morning. The sooner the better."

"All right, the soonest we have is April 12 at two-thirty."

My mother gasps. "Why do I have to wait that long? Shouldn't I do it right away?"

"Like I said, I am not at all concerned. You don't need to have this done right away. It is nothing. I am not worried. You really shouldn't be either. I am much more concerned about your osteoporosis."

We leave his office and I have no idea how she will survive the next three weeks until the biopsy. I am sure she doesn't have cancer. But for as long as I can remember cancer is the only thing she has feared. More than poverty, more than grief, more than estrangement, more than any sudden loop her life has thrown her for, except getting old. Getting old sucks. I know there must be some beauty in it, but at the moment it escapes me. After surviving this stinking life with all its disappointments shouldn't there be something better at the end than watching your body become a condemned property? The beautiful house in which you spent your youth, your summers, quiet evenings reading in a chair by the fire, hard times, holidays with loved ones, falls apart. And you still live there. The pipes burst, termites infiltrate the infrastructure, and there is not a single contractor in the world who can fix it.

In the elevator my mother swallows two handfuls of pills. She throws her head back to make sure they all go down.

"I want you to know," she says. "I have never been on more medication in my life. And I've never felt worse."

My friend Kerry is a better mother, more patient, gentler and more energetic than I. She is goodness personified. She is also a vegetarian and doesn't use wipes because even though they are convenient and the greatest invention since sliced bread, they are wasteful. She uses a menstrual cup for the same reason. She is kind to all humans, plants, and animals. I really think she is a modern-day saint.

Kerry works at a birthing center in a major hospital as a labor nurse. She works through the night on her hands and knees, bent over, covered in sweat, up to her elbows in placenta and women's shit. Her reward is the continued affirmation of the miracle that is life. She loves her work.

Two weeks ago, during a routine labor, a mother was rushed out of the birthing center for an emergency C-section. A drug that makes you forget was immediately administered, because there was no time to wait for anesthesia to take effect. She was wide awake when her baby was born dead. Kerry stayed with the family for hours after her shift. She visited them the next day, on her day off. She took the following day off, and another. She took a week off. She aged ten years. She went back to work yesterday and was transferred out of the birthing center to help with a delivery in the regular part of the hospital again. The baby was born healthy, seven pounds six ounces, but the mother died ten minutes before she ever had a chance to see her child. Kerry is in shock.

"I don't understand anything. I can't believe how many bad things there are in the world," she says when I meet her for coffee. She hasn't slept yet and it is hard to imagine she will anytime soon; the images of these two deaths weigh so heavy in her mind. "No one is safe. I am terrified. None of these people had any warning, Cathy, any time to prepare." Her voice is ten octaves lower. Tears fall down her face. These ideas are all new to her. Poor Kerry.

I, on the other hand, am defined by them. I have been educated in loss and death since I can remember. Death is my mother's specialty, my most treasured family heirloom.

"There is no security," I hear myself agree. "But I bet people would tell you that knowing, or being able to prepare, doesn't help." My sister's thirty-nine-year-old husband fell down dead one sunny September afternoon playing tennis in Central Park. Would her loss have been easier if she had been prepared? Would my mother's widowhood have been more palatable if she had had warning? Will I miss my ex-husband less because I have been warned? Will his daughter, his wife, his parents mourn him less? I don't think so. I have been preparing for my mother's death since high school. I have a copy of *The Magic Mountain* waiting for me. It is her favorite book and I haven't allowed myself to read it yet. But who am I kidding? It's not enough of a plan.

"We are all born and we all have to die," I say to Kerry, trying to distract myself from my past and impending grief. "It's just part of the arrangement. We have to experience both ends of the spectrum. There is incredible joy and incredible tragedy." I hear myself and I almost sound wise. I sound just like my mother. "All we have are moments of human contact. I am starting to think that is the meaning of life. Kindness is the only thing that doesn't go away. Even when people die." The last two years have put me face to face with my mother's mortality. I hope I can remember half of my own advice when I am lying prostrate on the ground empty and turned inside-out with grief because she is dead and I am an orphan.

My mother has become my best friend, the person I love to talk to most about books, about the state of the world, about grief, about everything. And she is going to die. I worry she will read this book and be upset. "Am I mean?" she said when I told her. "I just don't want to be mean. Oh well, never mind, it's your book. It's your take." Her generosity astounded me. Then she changed the subject and told me, "I'm finished."

"With what?" I asked.

"Being crazy. I'm alive for Christ's sake. I am getting older, I guess I'm getting old. I have to face it. But I am still alive and I realized it is just ludicrous. I may as well have a good time."

"Jesus, so you're done? You just pulled yourself together?"

"That's right. I might as well enjoy what time I have left."

I bet she will. I am the one in trouble because she is going to die.

I am not my mother. I don't know how to pull myself together. I have never gotten over anything.

Three weeks later the biopsy results are back. My mother does not have cancer. Her morbid preoccupation with death falls away, like layers of dry skin. She is exfoliated and new. She is glowing. We run down First Avenue to reach the little purple NYU trolley that will take us back downtown. She seems twenty years younger.

"Congratulations, you survived thyroid cancer," I say climbing aboard.

"Isn't it fabulous?" she says grinning, flashing her NYU ID to the driver.

"It sure is. Let's celebrate. Let me take you shopping. Or to get a manicure. You're going to live!"

"Oh Cathy. Okay let's have lunch, I guess." We get off the trolley and walk briskly to our favorite ramen counter. She is a different person.

"What do I want?" my mother asks me.

"I don't know, soup or vegetables?"

"Oh. Vegetables. I am so exhausted from this ordeal I could die. I have come home every night since the spa and gone to bed."

"It must be exhausting—planning your death," I say.

"It is," she assures me.

"You did the same thing with the osteoporosis and then with the high blood pressure. You thought you were going to lose your job. Freddy told you it was extremely mild and bound to happen to anyone who lives past seventy and that it was nothing to change your life about and you went straight home and planned your funeral."

"I know. That's what I do."

"Well, to quote you, 'Balance.'"

"I know," she says smiling. "I have none."

"Me neither. Thanks a lot." I look at her freckles, her blue eyes, and her face. Her features and her bone structure have become more defined, more delicate over the years and, I realize for the first time, prettier. I am sitting with my very pretty, beautiful mother. I want to touch her cheekbones with my fingertip; I want to memorize every square inch of her.

"You know the doorman? Your doorman retired. He's gone. They sent a card around for everyone to sign. But I wouldn't. I refused. I wouldn't do it." She says it without looking at me. I accept this as an apology without acknowledging it as such. We eat in silence for a little while, and then she says, "Phillip gave me a seven-hundred-and-fifty-dollar digital camera for my birthday. I have no idea how to use the fucking thing."

"He's rich."

"He certainly is. He is in another league. Beverly too. Beverly has a driver."

"So does my friend Julie, the sitcom star. She was in town last week. Her driver took us to galleries, out to dinner, and then dropped her off at the theater before being instructed to take me to as many bookstores as it took to find me a certain book she wants me to read."

"Beverly's driver picked me up last Thursday to take me to dinner. I think I don't mind being driven."

"I think I don't mind either," I say smiling. "And the whole time I was in the car I kept thinking how that was almost me. You know?"

"You were heading in that direction huh?" We drink our tea. "The one thing I do know," my mother says musing over her vegetables, "is you can't live through your children. They leave you and if you don't have a life without them, you're nowhere. Like my sister. And Pam Blaire. She turned down becoming a partner so she could be home with her kids on Friday nights and now look at her. They are in college and she is miserable."

"Isn't she miserable because her husband doesn't talk to her?" I know Pam Blaire's husband; he talks about sports and doesn't like to cuddle.

"Well if she was a partner maybe she wouldn't care."

"Maybe her relationship with her kids makes her very happy. Some people get a lot of pleasure being with their kids, you know what I mean?"

"Maybe. But I sure am grateful I have my job. I'm nothing without my job," my mother says, and truer words could not be said.

"I guess I'm lucky," I say. "I mean I have a job I love, but I can do it when I want. I still get to be with Olive and delude myself that I have a career. I don't make any money—that's where the fantasy falls short—but it's still the best job I ever had. You know what I mean?"

"God, Cathy. You have got to stop saying that."

"Well, do you know what I mean?"

"It is less important that I know what you mean than that you sound intelligent," she tells me and pays the check.

The warmth of the April sun is making its way down to us on earth and the birds are happy and the ground around the trees is studded with daffodils. My mother celebrated her birthday last week and I will celebrate mine in six days and I am enchanted, as I am every year that winter is finally over and there is color and warmth again in the world.

"Mom, let's do something. I want to take you somewhere. Let's celebrate."

"We just had lunch," she says.

"I know. But I really want to take you somewhere. Shopping, to get a manicure, a massage, something. To celebrate."

"I don't like any of those things, Cathy," she says.

"I know. But you're my mother and you are very much alive. I feel like something is in order. Can I take you to Bloomingdale's and buy you something like you always used to do for me?"

"Cathy . . ."

"Please?"

"I just really want to go back to the office," she says.

On the corner of Broadway and Waverly we stand in front of the building that has been her real home for the last thirty-three years.

I hug her, probably too tight, and send her on her way.

ACKNOWLEDGMENTS

Once upon a time I wrote four-
teen pages about traveling to Paris with my mother. I read it at a
reading series and then promptly put it in a drawer. I would like to
thank Naked Angels Tuesdays at Nine for initiating those fourteen
pages and then giving me the opportunity ten years later to turn
them into something I could take out of the drawer. I would especially like to thank Liz Benjamin, for her remarkable support and
encouragement. A writer never had a better and more generous
champion than she. I would also like to thank Joe Danisi and
Stephanie Cannon for carrying on the nurturing that Liz began.
Thank you to Jen Albano for suggesting I read something there,
which inadvertently got me to begin this book. Thank you Sharr
White for telling me that what I was doing was writing a book; I really didn't know. I would also like to thank all the people who came
to Tuesdays and were so good to listen to so much of this mater-
ial—especially Jeanne Dorsey and Daniel Rietz. I would like to
thank Wendy Burns for reading every single miserable draft there
ever was. And tons of thanks to Eric Chinski, the ever lovely Gena
Hamshaw, Lorin Stein, and everyone at FSG who has been so wonderful. To Theo Leiber, for introducing me to the incredible Sarah
Burnes, and Sarah Burnes, for being the greatest agent and lady and

supermom I know. And to Jessica Craig for so much hard work. I want to thank Ayesha Pande for gently and insistently prodding me to write more and more and more. Chris Lamb for being cool as a cucumber, there in a pinch, and generally perfect. Sara Tucek, Robyn Mundell, Shannon Timms, and Michael Showalter for so much encouragement and for reading such early incarnations. Maggie Levine, Brooke Watkins, Jessie Allen, and Catherine Coy for reading early drafts and not telling me to put it back in the drawer. Scott Coffey and Blair Mastbaum for reading and reading. Jessica Blatt and Sean Jacobs for being good friends. Deven Golden for art class 101. Tom and Bonnie Forgash who stepped in as my nanny, cook, and laundresses when I had deadlines. David Rakoff for showing me how classy and wonderful and generous the world of publishing can be, because he is so classy and wonderful and generous. Alexandra Fuller for giving me something to aspire to. Paul Bravmann for helping me every single step of the way; I could not have done it without him, at all. I owe him plenty. Adam Forgash for helping me and helping me and helping me and living with me and still loving me and helping me some more and still loving me. The beautiful Olive Bernard Forgash for teaching me most of what I have learned over the last five years. And mostly my mother, without whom none of this would be possible.